Say It Right in FRENCH

Easily Pronounced Language Systems, Inc.

INFINITE Destinations, ONE Pronunciation System

New York Chicago San Francisco Lisbon London Madrid Mexico City
Milan New Delhi San Juan Seoul Singapore Sydney Toronto

The McGraw·Hill Companies

Library of Congress Cataloging-in-Publication Data

Say it right in French / by Easily Pronounced Language Systems.
p. cm. — (Say it right)
Includes index.
ISBN 0-07-146916-8
1. French language—Pronunciation. I. Easily Pronounced Language Systems. II. Series.

PC2137.S39 2006
448.3'421—dc22 2005058353

4 5 6 7 8 9 10 11 12 13 14 15 16 17 18 19 20 21 LBM/LBM 0 9 8 7

ISBN 978-0-07-146916-6
MHID 0-07-146916-8

McGraw-Hill books are available at special quantity discounts to use as premiums and sales promotions, or for use in corporate training programs. For more information, please write to the Director of Special Sales, Professional Publishing, McGraw-Hill, Two Penn Plaza, New York, NY 10121-2298. Or contact your local bookstore.

Also available:

Dígalo correctamente en inglés (Say It Right in English)
Say It Right in Chinese
Say It Right in German
Say It Right in Italian
Say It Right in Japanese
Say It Right in Spanish

Author: Clyde Peters
Illustrations: Luc Nisset

Acknowledgments

Betty Chapman, President, EPLS Corporation
Priscilla Leal Bailey, Senior Series Editor

This book is printed on acid-free paper.

CONTENTS

INTRODUCTION

The SAY IT RIGHT FOREIGN LANGUAGE PHRASE BOOK SERIES has been developed with the conviction that learning to speak a foreign language should be fun and easy!

All SAY IT RIGHT phrase books feature the EPLS Vowel Symbol System, a revolutionary phonetic system that stresses consistency, clarity, and above all, simplicity!

Since this unique phonetic system is used in all SAY IT RIGHT phrase books, you only have to learn the VOWEL SYMBOL SYSTEM ONCE!

The SAY IT RIGHT series uses the easiest phrases possible for English speakers to pronounce and is designed to reflect how foreign languages are used by native speakers.

You will be amazed at how confidence in your pronunciation leads to an eagerness to talk to other people in their own language.

Whether you want to learn a new language for travel, education, business, study, or personal enrichment, SAY IT RIGHT phrase books offer a simple and effective method of pronunciation and communication.

PRONUNCIATION GUIDE

Most English speakers are familiar with the French word **Merci**. This is how the correct pronunciation is represented in the EPLS Vowel Symbol System.

All French vowel sounds are assigned a specific non-changing symbol. When these symbols are used in conjunction with consonants and read normally, pronunciation of even the most difficult foreign word becomes incredibly EASY.

On the following page are all the EPLS Vowel Symbols used in this book. They are EASY to LEARN since their sounds are familiar. Beneath each symbol are three English words which contain the sound of the symbol.

Practice pronouncing the words under each symbol until you mentally associate the correct vowel sound with the correct symbol. Most symbols are pronounced the way they look!

THE SAME BASIC SYMBOLS ARE USED IN ALL SAY IT RIGHT PHRASE BOOKS!

EPLS VOWEL SYMBOL SYSTEM

(A)	(EE)	(O)	(oo)
Ace	S**ee**	**O**ak	C**oo**l
B**a**ke	F**ee**t	C**o**ld	P**oo**l
S**a**fe	M**ee**t	S**o**ld	T**oo**

(ă)	(ĕ)	(ah)	(uh)
C**a**t	M**e**n	M**o**m	F**u**n
S**a**d	R**e**d	H**o**t	S**u**n
H**a**t	B**e**d	**O**ff	R**u**n

(ew)

N**ew**
F**ew**
D**ew**

This symbol represents the French letter **u**. Put your lips together as if to kiss and say **EE**.

(ou)

C**ou**ld
W**ou**ld
B**oo**k

This symbol represents a unique sound found in the letters **eu** in French spelling. To master this sound you must listen to a native speaker's pronunciation. The **ou** sound in c**ou**ld is an effective substitute.

EPLS CONSONANTS

Consonants are letters like **T**, **D**, and **K**. They are easy to recognize and their pronunciation seldom changes. The following pronunciation guide letters represent some unique French consonant sounds.

R̰ Represents the French **r**. Try to pronounce it far back in the throat. Listen to a native speaker to master this sound.

ZH Pronounce these EPLS letters like the **s** in mea**s**ure.

KW Pronounce these EPLS letters like the **qu** in **qu**it.

Nasalized Vowel Sounds

In French certain vowels are nasalized. This (**ñ**) immediately following a symbol tells you to nasalize the sound that the symbol represents. Try pinching your nose while pronouncing these words (try not to sound the **n** in the words):

Can	Zone	On	Sun
K(ă)ñ	Z(O)ñ	(ah)ñ	S(uh)ñ

PRONUNCIATION TIPS

- Each pronunciation guide word is broken into syllables. Read each word slowly, one syllable at a time, increasing speed as you become more familiar with the system.
- In general, equal emphasis is given to each syllable. Sometimes the French will slightly stress the last syllable in a sentence.
- Most of the symbols are pronounced the way they look!
- This phrase book provides a means to speak and be understood in French. To perfect your French accent you must listen closely to French speakers and adjust your speech accordingly.
- The pronunciation and word choices in this book were chosen for their simplicity and effectiveness.
- Some pronunciation guide letters are underlined (**Z** T **N**). This is simply to let you know that the underlined letter is a linking sound which appears to separate two vowel sounds.
- **SVP** is the abbreviation for **s'il vous plaît** which means "please" in French. You will see it used throughout the book.

ICONS USED IN THIS BOOK

KEY WORDS

You will find this icon at the beginning of chapters indicating key words relating to chapter content. These are important words to become familiar with.

PHRASEMAKER

The Phrasemaker icon provides the traveler with a choice of phrases that allows the user to make his or her own sentences.

Say It Right in FRENCH

ESSENTIAL WORDS AND PHRASES

Here are some basic words and phrases that will help you express your needs and feelings in French.

Hello

Bonjour

BⓄñ ZH⊚R

How are you?

Comment allez-vous?

KⓄ-MⓄñ T̲ⓐⓗ-LⒶ-V⊚

Fine / Very well

Très bien

TRⒶ BⒺ-ⓐ̆ñ

And you?

Et vous?

Ⓐ V⊚

Good-bye

Au revoir

Ⓞ Rⓤⓗ-VWⓐⓗR

Good morning

Bonjour

B(O)ñ ZH(oo)R

Good evening

Bonsoir

B(O)ñ SW(ah)R

Good night

Bonne nuit

B(uh)N NW(EE)

Mr.

Monsieur

M(uh)-SY(ou)

Mrs.

Madame

M(ah)-D(ah)M

Miss

Mademoiselle

M(ah)D-MW(ah)-Z(ĕ)L

Yes

Oui

W(EE)

No

Non

N(O)ñ

Please

S'il vous plaît

S(EE)L V(OO) PL(ĕ)

Abbreviated SVP throughout book

Thank you

Merci

M(ĕ)R-S(EE)

Excuse me

Pardon

P(ah)R-D(O)ñ

I'm sorry

Je suis désolé

ZH(uh) SW(EE) D(A)-S(O)-L(A)

I'm a tourist.

Je suis touriste.

ZH(uh) SW(EE) T(oo)-R(EE)ST

I do not speak French.

Je ne parle pas français.

ZH(uh)N-(uh) P(ah)RL P(ah) FR(ah)ñ-S(A)

I speak a little French.

Je parle un peu français.

ZH(uh) P(ah)RL (uh)ñ P(ou) FR(ah)ñ-S(A)

Do you understand English?

Comprenez-vous anglais?

K(O)ñ-PR(uh)-N(A) V(oo) (ah)ñ-GL(A)

I don't understand!

Je ne comprends pas!

ZH(uh)N-(uh) K(O)ñ-PR(ah)ñ P(ah)

Please repeat.

Répétez s'il vous plaît.

R(A)-P(A)-T(A) S(EE)L V(oo) PL(e)

FEELINGS

I want...

Je veux...

ZH(uh) V(ou)...

I have...

J'ai...

ZH(A)...

I know.

Je sais.

ZH(uh) S(A)

I don't know.

Je ne sais pas.

ZH(uh)N S(A) P(ah)

I like it.

Je l'aime bien.

ZH(uh) L(ĕ)M B(EE)-(ă)ñ

I don't like it.

Je ne l'aime pas bien.

ZH(uh)N-(uh) L(ĕ)M P(ah) B(EE)-(ă)ñ

I'm lost.

Je suis perdu.

ZH(uh) SW(EE) P(ĕ)R-D(ew)

I'm in a hurry.

Je suis pressé.

ZH(uh) SW(EE) PR(ĕ)-S(A)

I'm tired.

Je suis fatigué.

ZH(uh) SW(EE) F(ah)-T(EE)-G(A)

I'm ill.

Je suis malade.

ZH(uh) SW(EE) M(ah)-L(ah)D

I'm hungry.

J'ai faim.

ZH(A) F(ă)ñ

I'm thirsty.

J'ai soif.

ZH(A) SW(ah)F

I'm angry.

Je suis en colère.

ZH(uh) SW(EE) Z(ah)ñ K(O)-L(ĕ)R

INTRODUCTIONS

My name is...

Je m'appelle...

ZH(uh) M(ah)-P(ĕ)L...

What's your name?

Comment vous appelez-vous?

K(O)-M(O)ñ V(oo) Z(ah)-PL(A) V(oo)

Where are you from?

D'où venez-vous?

D(oo) V(uh)-N(A) V(oo)

Do you live here?

Habitez-vous ici?

(ah)-B(EE)-T(A) V(oo) Z(EE)-S(EE)

I just arrived.

Je viens d'arriver.

ZH(uh) V(EE)-(ă)ñ D(ah)-R(EE)-V(A)

What hotel are you [staying] at?

Vous restez à quel hôtel?

V(oo) R(ĕ)S-T(A) (ah) K(ĕ) L(O)-T(ĕ)L

I'm at the...hotel.

Je reste à l'hôtel...

ZH(uh) R(ĕ)ST (ah) L(O)-T(ĕ)L...

It was nice to meet you.

Je suis enchanté de faire votre connaissance.

ZH(uh) SW(EE) Z(ah)ñ-SH(ah)ñ-T(A)
D(uh) F(ĕ)R V(O)-TR(uh)
K(O)-N(A)-S(ah)ñS

See you tomorrow.

A demain.

(ah) D(uh)-M(ă)ñ

See you later.

A bientôt.

(ah) B(EE)-(ă)ñ-T(O)

Good luck!

Bonne chance!

B(uh)N SH(ah)ñS

In this book the symbol (uh) is used to represent the French letter "**e**" in words such as **le, de,** etc. To master your French accent, have a French speaker pronounce these words and try to hone your accent accordingly.

THE BIG QUESTION

Who?

Qui?

K(EE)

Who is it?

Qui est-ce?

K(EE) (ĕ)S

What?

Quoi? Comment?

KW(ah) K(O)-M(O)ñ

What's that?

Qu'est-ce que c'est?

K(ĕ)S-K(uh) S(A)

When?

Quand?

K(ah)ñ

Where?

Où?

(oo)

Where is...?

Où est...?

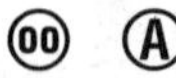

Which?

Quel? Quelle? Quels? Quelles?

K(ĕ)L

Although spelled differently these are all pronounced the same.

Why?

Pourquoi?

P(oo)R KW(ah)

How?

Comment?

K(O)-M(O)ñ

How much does it cost?

Combien?

K(O)ñ-B(EE)-(ă)ñ

How long?

Combien de temps?

K(O)ñ-B(EE)-(ă)ñ D(uh) T(ah)ñ

ASKING FOR THINGS

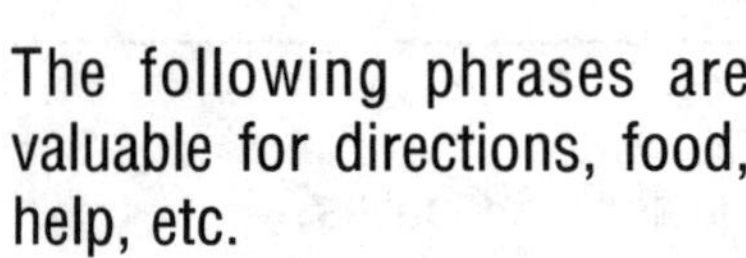

The following phrases are valuable for directions, food, help, etc.

I would like...

Je voudrais...

ZH(uh) V(oo)-DR(A)...

I need...?

J'ai besoin...?

ZH(A) B(uh)-ZW(ă)ñ...

Can you...

Pouvez-vous...

P(oo)-V(A)-V(oo)...

When asking for things be sure to say please and thank you.

Please	Thank you
S'il vous plaît	Merci
S(EE)L V(oo) PL(ĕ)	M(ĕ)R-S(EE)

PHRASEMAKER

Combine **I would like** with the following phrases beneath, and you will have a good idea how to ask for things.

I would like...

Je voudrais...

ZH(uh) V(oo)-DR(A)... SVP

▸ **more coffee**

plus de café

PL(ew) D(uh) K(ah)-F(A)

▸ **some water**

de l'eau

D(uh) L(O)

▸ **some ice**

de la glace

D(uh) L(ah) GL(ah)S

▸ **the menu**

le menu

L(uh) M(ĕ)-N(ew)

PHRASEMAKER

Here are a few sentences you can use when you feel the urge to say **I need**... or **Can you**...?

I need...

J'ai besoin...

ZHⒶ B(uh)-ZW(ă)ñ...

▸ **help**

d'aide

D(ĕ)D

▸ **directions**

de directions

D(uh) D(EE)-R(ĕ)K-S(EE)-Ⓞñ

▸ **more money**

de plus d'argent

D(uh) PL(ew) D(ah)R-ZH(ah)ñ

▸ **change**

de monnaie

D(uh) MⓄ-NⒶ

▸ **a lawyer**

d'un avocat

D(uh)ñ N(ah)-VⓄ-K(ah)

PHRASEMAKER

Can you...

Pouvez-vous...

P(oo)-V(A)-V(oo)...

- **help me?**

  m'aider?

  M(A)-D(A)

- **show me?**

  me montrer?

  M(uh) M(O)ñ-TR(A)

- **give me...?**

  me donner...?

  M(uh) D(O)-N(A)...

- **tell me...?**

  me dire...?

  M(uh) D(EE)R...

- **take me to...?**

  m'emmener...?

  M(uh)M-N(A)...

ASKING THE WAY

No matter how independent you are, sooner or later you'll probably have to ask for directions.

Where is...?

Où est...?

(oo) Ⓐ...

Is it near?

C'est près d'ici?

SⒶ PRⒶ D(EE)-S(EE)

Is it far?

C'est loin d'ici?

SⒶ LW(ă)ñ D(EE)-S(EE)

I'm lost!

Je suis perdu!

ZH(uh) SW(EE) P(ĕ)R-D(ew)

I'm looking for...

Je cherche...

ZH(uh) SH(ĕ)RSH...

PHRASEMAKER

Where is...

Où est...

(oo) (A)...

- **the restroom?**

  la toilette?

  L(ah) TW(ah)-L(ĕ)T

- **the telephone?**

  le téléphone?

  L(uh) T(A)-L(A)-F(O)N

- **the beach?**

  la plage?

  L(ah) PL(ah)ZH

- **the hotel...?**

  l'hôtel...?

  L(O)-T(ĕ)L...

- **the train for...?**

  le train à...?

  L(uh) TR(ă)ñ (ah)...

TIME

What time is it?

Quelle heure est-il?

K(ĕ) L(ou)R (A)-T(EE)L

Morning

Le matin

L(uh) M(ah)-T(ă)ñ

Noon

Midi

M(EE)-D(EE)

Night

La nuit

L(ah) NW(EE)

Today

Aujourd'hui

(O)-ZH(oo)R-DW(EE)

Tomorrow

Demain

D(uh)-M(ă)ñ

This week

Cette semaine

S(ĕ)T S(uh)-M(ĕ)N

This month

Ce mois

S(uh) MW(ah)

This year

Cette année

S(ĕ)T (ah)-N(A)

Now

Maintenant

M(ă)ñ-T(uh)-N(ah)ñ

Soon

Bientôt

B(EE)-(ă)ñ-T(O)

Later

Plus tard

PL(ew) T(ah)R

Never

Jamais

ZH(ah)-M(A)

WHO IS IT?

I

Je

ZH(uh)

You (Formal)

Vous

V(oo)

Use this form of **you** with people you don't know well.

You (Informal)

Tu

T(ew)

Use this form of **you** with people you know well.

We

Nous

N(oo)

They

Ils (m)

(EE)L

A group of **men** only or a group of men and women.

Elles (f)

(ĕ)L

A group of **women** only.

THE, A (AN), AND SOME

To use the correct form of **The**, **A** (**An**), or **Some**, you must know if the French word is masculine or feminine. Often you will have to guess! If you make a mistake, you will still be understood.

The

La L(ah) **The** before a singular feminine noun: (La) woman is pretty.	Les L(A) **The** before a plural feminine noun: (Les) women are pretty.
Le L(uh) **The** before a singular masculine noun: (Le) man is handsome.	Les L(A) **The** before a plural masculine noun: (Les) men are handsome.

A or An

Un (uh)ñ **A** or **an** before a singular masculine noun: He is (un) man.	Une (ew)N **A** or **an** before a singular feminine noun: She is (une) woman.

Some

Du D(ew) **Some** before singular masculine nouns: (Du) men.	De la D(uh) L(ah) **Some** before singular feminine nouns: (De la) women.

USEFUL OPPOSITES

Near	**Far**
Près	Loin
PR(A)	LW(ă)ñ
Here	**There**
Ici	Là
(EE)-S(EE)	L(ah)
Left	**Right**
A gauche	A droite
(ah) G(O)SH	(ah) DRW(ah)T
A little	**A lot**
Un peu	Beaucoup
(uh)ñ P(ou)	B(O)-K(oo)
More	**Less**
Plus	Moins
PL(ew)	MW(ă)ñ
Big	**Small**
Grand (m), Grande (f)	Petit (m), Petite (f)
GR(ah)ñ, GR(ah)ND	P(uh)-T(EE), P(uh)-T(EE)T

Adjectives are masculine or feminine depending on the noun they describe.

Open	**Closed**
Ouvert (m), Ouverte (f)	Fermé (m), Fermée (f)
(oo)-V(ĕ)R, (oo)-V(ĕ)RT	F(ĕ)R-MⒶ
Cheap	**Expensive**
Bon marché	Cher (m), Chère (f)
BⓄñ M(ah)R-SHⒶ	SH(ĕ)R
Clean	**Dirty**
Propre	Sale
PRⓄ-PR(uh)	S(ah)L
Good	**Bad**
Bon (m), Bonne (f)	Mauvais (m), Mauvaise (f)
BⓄñ, B(uh)N	MⓄ-VⒶ, MⓄ-V(ĕ)Z
Vacant	**Occupied**
Libre	Occupé (m), Occupée (f)
L(EE)-BR(uh)	Ⓞ-K(oo)-PⒶ
Right	**Wrong**
Avoir raison	Avoir tort
(ah)-VW(ah)R RⒶ-ZⓄñ	(ah)-VW(ah)R TⓄR

WORDS OF ENDEARMENT

I love you.

Je t'aime.

ZH(uh) T(ĕ)M

My love

Mon amour

M(O)ñ N(ah)-M(oo)R

My life

Ma vie

M(ah) V(EE)

My friend (to a male)

Mon ami (m)

M(O)ñ N(ah)-M(EE)

My friend (to a female)

Mon amie (f)

M(O)ñ N(ah)-M(EE)

Kiss me!

Embrasse-moi!

(ah)ñ-BR(ah)S MW(ah)

WORDS OF ANGER

What do you want?

Qu'est-ce que vous voulez?

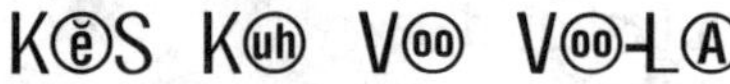

Leave me alone!

Laissez-moi tranquille!

LA-SA MWah TRahñ-KEEL

Go away!

Allez-vous-en!

ah-LA Voo-Zahñ

Stop bothering me!

Ne me dérangez pas!

Nuh Muh DA-Rahñ-ZHA Pah

Be quiet!

Taisez-vous!

TA-ZA Voo

That's enough!

C'est assez!

SA Tah-SA

COMMON EXPRESSIONS

When you are at a loss for words but have the feeling you should say something, try one of these!

Who knows?

Qui sait?

K(EE) S(A)

That's the truth!

C'est la vérité!

S(A) L(ah) V(A)-R(EE)-T(A)

Sure!

Bien sûr!

B(EE)-(ă)ñ S(ew)R

Wow!

Chouette!

SH(oo)-(ĕ)T

What's happening?

Qu'est-ce qui se passe?

K(ĕ)S K(EE) S(uh) P(ah)S

I think so.

Je pense que oui.

ZH(uh) P(ah)ñS K(uh) W(EE)

Cheers!

A votre santé!

ⓐⓗ VⓄ-TRⓤⓗ Sⓐⓗñ-TⒶ

Good luck!

Bonne chance!

BⓤⓗN SHⓐⓗñS

With pleasure!

Avec plaisir!

ⓐⓗ-Vⓔ̆K PLⒶ-ZⒺⒺR

My goodness!

Mon dieu!

MⓄñ DYⓞⓤ

What a shame! / That's too bad!

C'est dommage!

SⒶ DⓄ-MⓐⓗZH

Well done! Bravo!

Bravo!

BRⓐⓗ-VⓄ

Never mind!

N'importe quoi!

Nⓐ̆ñ-PⓄRT KWⓐⓗ

USEFUL COMMANDS

Stop!

Arrêtez!

Go!

Allez!

ah-LA

Wait!

Attendez!

ah-Tahñ-DA

Hurry!

Dépêchez-vous!

DA-Pĕ-SHA Voo

Slow down!

Lentement!

Lahñ-Tuh-Mahñ

Come here!

Venez ici!

Vuh-NA ZEE-SEE

Help!

Au secours!

O Suh-KooR

EMERGENCIES

Fire!

Au feu!

Ⓞ F(ou)

Emergency!

L'urgence!

L(ew)R-ZH(ah)ñS

Call the police!

Téléphonez au police!

TⒶ-LⒶ-FⓄ-NⒶ Ⓞ PⓄ-L(EE)S

Call a doctor!

Téléphonez au médecin!

TⒶ-LⒶ-FⓄ-NⒶ Ⓞ MⒶ-D(uh)-S(ă)ñ

Call an ambulance!

Faites venir une ambulance!

F(ĕ)T V(uh)-N(EE)R (ew)N (ah)ñ-B(ew)-L(ah)ñS

I need help!

Au secours!

Ⓞ S(uh)-K(oo)R

ARRIVAL

Passing through customs should be easy since there are usually agents available who speak English. You may be asked how long you intend to stay and if you have anything to declare.

- Have your passport ready.
- Be sure all documents are up-to-date.
- While in a foreign country, it is wise to keep receipts for everything you buy.
- Be aware that many countries will charge a departure tax when you leave. Your travel agent should be able to find out if this affects you.
- If you have connecting flights, be sure to reconfirm them in advance.
- Make sure your luggage is clearly marked inside and out.
- Take valuables and medicines in carry-on bags.

SIGNS TO LOOK FOR:

DOUANE (Customs)

FRONTIERE (Border)

LES BAGAGES (Baggage claim)

KEY WORDS

Baggage

Les bagages

L(A) B(ah)-G(ah)ZH

Customs

La douane

L(ah) DW(ah)N

Documents

Les documents

L(A) D(O)-K(oo)-M(ah)ñ

Passport

Le passeport

L(uh) P(ah)S-P(O)R

Porter

Le porteur

L(uh) P(O)R-T(ou)R

Tax

La taxe

L(ah) T(ah)KS

USEFUL PHRASES

Here is my passport.

Voici mon passeport.

VW(ah)-S(EE) M(O)ñ P(ah)S-P(O)R

I have nothing to declare.

Je n'ai rien à déclarer.

ZH(uh) N(A) R(EE)-(ă)ñ (ah)
D(A)-KL(ah)-R(A)

I'm on business.

Je suis en voyage d'affaires.

ZH(uh) SW(EE) Z(ah)ñ VW(ah)-Y(ah)ZH
D(ah)-F(ĕ)R

I'm on vacation.

Je suis en vacances.

ZH(uh) SW(EE) Z(ah)ñ V(ah)-K(ah)ñS

Is there a problem?

Il y a un problème?

(EE)L (EE) (ah) (uh)ñ PR(O)-BL(ĕ)M

PHRASEMAKER

I'll be staying...

Je vais rester...

ZH(uh) V(A) R(ĕ)S-T(A)...

- **one week**

  une semaine

  (ew)N S(uh)-M(ĕ)N

- **two weeks**

  deux semaines

  D(ou) S(uh)-M(ĕ)N

- **one month**

  un mois

  (uh)ñ MW(ah)

- **two months**

  deux mois

  D(ou) MW(ah)

USEFUL PHRASES

I need a porter!

J'ai besoin d'un porteur!

ZH(A) B(uh)-ZW(ă)ñ D(uh)ñ P(O)R-T(ou)R

These are my bags.

Voici mes bagages.

VW(ah)-S(EE) M(A) B(ah)-G(ah)ZH

I'm missing a bag.

Je manque une valise.

ZH(uh) M(ah)ñ K(ew)N V(ah)-L(EE)S

Take my bags to the taxi, please.

Prenez mes valises au taxi, s'il vous plaît.

PR(uh)-N(A) M(A) V(ah)-L(EE)S (O)
T(ah)K-S(EE) SVP

Thank you. This is for you.

Merci. C'est pour vous.

M(ĕ)R-S(EE) S(A) P(oo)R V(oo)

PHRASEMAKER

Where is...

Ou est...

Ⓞⓞ Ⓐ...

- **customs?**

  la douane?

  LⓐⓗDWⓐⓗN

- **baggage claim?**

  le depot de bagages?

  Lⓤⓗ DⒶ-PⓄ Dⓤⓗ Bⓐⓗ-GⓐⓗZH

- **the money exchange?**

  le bureau d'échange?

  Lⓤⓗ Bⓔⓦ-RⓄ DⒶ-SHⓐⓗñZH

- **the taxi stand?**

  la station de taxi?

  Lⓐⓗ STⓐⓗ-SⒺⒺ-Ⓞñ Dⓤⓗ TⓐⓗK-SⒺⒺ

- **the bus stop?**

  l'arrêt d'autobus?

  Lⓐⓗ-Rⓔ̆ DⓄ-TⓄ-BⓔⓦS

HOTEL SURVIVAL

A wide selection of accommodations, ranging from the most basic to the most extravagant, are available wherever you travel in France. When booking your room, find out what amenities are included for the price you pay.

- Make reservations well in advance and get written confirmation of your reservations before you leave home.
- Always have identification ready when checking in.
- Do not leave valuables, prescriptions, or cash in your room when you are not there!
- Electrical items like blow-dryers may need an adapter. Your hotel may be able to provide one, but to be safe, take one with you.
- **Service Compris** or **Toutes Taxes Comprises** on your bill means the tip is already included, except for the bellman.

KEY WORDS

Hotel

L'hôtel

Ⓛ-T ⓔL

L⓪-TⓔL

Bellman

Un garçon d'hôtel

ⓤⓗñ GⓐⓗR-S⓪ñ D⓪-TⓔL

Maid

Une domestique

ⓔⓦN D⓪-MⓔS-TⓔⓔK

Message

Le message

Lⓤⓗ Mⓔ-SⓐⓗZH

Reservation

La réservation

Lⓐⓗ RⒶ-SⓔR-Vⓐⓗ-Sⓔⓔ-⓪ñ

Room service

Le service dans les chambres

Lⓤⓗ SⓔR-VⓔⓔS Dⓐⓗñ LⒶ SHⓐⓗñ-BRⓤⓗ

CHECKING IN

My name is...

Je m'appelle...

ZH(uh) M(ah)-P(ĕ)L

I have a reservation.

J'ai réservé.

ZH(A) R(A)-S(ĕ)R-V(A)

Have you any vacancies?

Vous avez des chambres libres?

V(oo) Z̲(ah)-V(A) D(A) SH(ah)ñ-BR(uh) L(EE)-BR(uh)

What is the charge?

Quel est le prix?

K(ĕ) L̲(A) L(uh) PR(EE)

Is there room service?

Il y a le service dans les chambres?

(EE)L (EE) (ah) L(uh) S(ĕ)R-V(EE)S D(ah)ñ L(A) SH(ah)ñ-BR(uh)

PHRASEMAKER

I would like a room...

Je voudrais une chambre...

ZH(uh) V(oo)-DR(A) (ew)N SH(ah)ñ-BR(uh)...

- **with a bath**

  avec une salle de bains

  (ah)-V(ĕ)K (ew)N S(ah)L D(uh) B(ă)ñ

- **with one bed**

  à un lit

  (ah) (uh)ñ L(EE)

- **with two beds**

  à deux lits

  (ah) D(ou) L(EE)

- **with a shower**

  avec une douche

  (ah)-V(ĕ)K (ew)N D(oo)SH

- **with a view**

  avec la vue

  (ah)-V(ĕ)K L(ah) V(ew)

USEFUL PHRASES

Where is the dining room?

Où est la salle à manger?

ⓞⓞ Ⓐ Lⓐⓗ Sⓐⓗ L ⓐⓗ Mⓐⓗñ-ZHⒶ

Are meals included?

Est-ce que les repas sont compris?

ⓔ̆S-Kⓤⓗ LⒶ Rⓤⓗ-Pⓐⓗ SⓄñ KⓄñ-PRⒺⒺ

What time is breakfast?

A quelle heure est le petit déjeuner?

ⓐⓗ Kⓔ̆ L̲ⓞⓤR Ⓐ Lⓤⓗ Pⓤⓗ-TⒺⒺ DⒶ-ZHⓞⓤ-NⒶ

What time is lunch?

A quelle heure est le déjeuner?

ⓐⓗ Kⓔ̆ L̲ⓞⓤR Ⓐ Lⓤⓗ DⒶ-ZHⓞⓤ-NⒶ

What time is dinner?

A quelle heure est le dîner?

ⓐⓗ Kⓔ̆ L̲ⓞⓤR Ⓐ Lⓤⓗ DⒺⒺ-NⒶ

My room key, please.

Ma clé de chambre, s'il vous plaît.

M(ah) KL(A) D(uh) SH(ah)ñ-BR(uh) SVP

Are there any messages for me?

Y a-t-il des messages pour moi?

(EE) (ah) T(EE)L D(A) M(ĕ)-S(ah)ZH P(oo)R MW(ah)

Please wake me at...

Veuillez me réveiller à...

V(ou)-Y(A) M(uh) R(A)-V(A)-Y(A) (ah)...

6:00	**6:30**
six heures	six heures et demie
S(EE) Z(ou)R	S(EE) Z(ou)R Z(A) D(uh)-M(EE)
7:00	**7:30**
sept heures	sept heures et demie
S(ĕ) T(ou)R	S(ĕ) T(ou)R Z(A) D(uh)-M(EE)
8:00	**8:30**
huit heures	huit heures et demie
W(EE) T(ou)R	W(EE) T(ou)R Z(A) D(uh)-M(EE)
9:00	**9:30**
neuf heures	neuf heures et demie
N(ou) V(ou)R	N(ou) V(ou)R Z(A) D(uh)-M(EE)

PHRASEMAKER

I need...

J'ai besoin...

ZHⒶ B(uh)-ZW(ă)ñ...

▸ **a babysitter**

d'une garde-bébé

D(ew)N G(ah)RD BⒶ-BⒶ

▸ **a bellman**

d'un garçon d'hôtel

D(uh)ñ G(ah)R-SⓄñ DⓄ-T(ĕ)L

▸ **more blankets**

de plus de couvertures

D(uh) PL(ew) D(uh) K(oo)-V(ĕ)R-T(ew)R

▸ **a hotel safe**

d'un coffre-fort

D(uh)ñ KⓄ-FR(uh) FⓄR

▸ **ice cubes**

de glaçons

D(uh) GL(ah)-SⓄñ

▸ **an extra key**

d'un clé supplémentaire

D(uh)ñ KLⒶ S(ew)-PLⒶ-M(uh)ñ-T(ĕ)R

▸ **a maid**

de domestique

D(uh) DⓄ-M(ĕ)S-T(EE)K

▸ **the manager**

de directeur (m) la directrice (f)

D(uh) D(EE)-R(ĕ)K-T(ou)R L(ah) D(EE)-R(ĕ)K-TR(EE)S

▸ **clean sheets**

de draps propres

D(uh) DR(ah) PRⓄ-PR(uh)

▸ **soap**

de savon

D(uh) S(ah)-VⓄñ

▸ **toilet paper**

de papier hygiénique

D(uh) P(ah)-P(EE)-Ⓐ (EE)-ZH(EE)-Ⓐ-N(EE)K

▸ **more towels**

de plus de serviettes

D(uh) PL(ew) D(uh) S(ĕ)R-V(EE)-(ĕ)T

PHRASEMAKER
(PROBLEMS)

There is no...

Il n'y a pas...

ⒺⒺL NYⓐⓗ Pⓐⓗ...

▸ **electricity**

d'électricité

DⒶ L🅔K-TRⒺⒺ-SⒺⒺ-TⒶ

▸ **heat**

de chauffage

Dⓤⓗ SHⓄ-FⓐⓗZH

▸ **hot water**

d'eau chaude

DⓄ SHⓄD

▸ **light**

de lumière

Dⓤⓗ LⓄⓄM-Y🅔R

▸ **toilet paper**

de papier hygiénique

Dⓤⓗ Pⓐⓗ-PⒺⒺ-Ⓐ ⒺⒺ-ZHⒺⒺ-Ⓐ-NⒺⒺK

PHRASEMAKER
(SPECIAL NEEDS)

Do you have...

Avez-vous...

ⓐⓗ-VⒶ Vⓞⓞ...

▸ **an elevator?**

un ascenseur?

ⓤⓗñ N̲ⓐⓗ-Sⓐⓗñ-SⓞⓤR

▸ **a ramp?**

une rampe?

ⓔⓦN RⓐⓗMP

▸ **a wheelchair?**

un fauteuil roulant?

ⓤⓗñ FⓄ-Tⓞⓤ-Yⓤⓗ Rⓞⓞ-Lⓐⓗñ

▸ **facilities for the disabled?**

des aménagements pour les handicapés?

DⒶ Z̲ⓐⓗ-MⒶ-NⓐⓗZH-Mⓐⓗñ PⓞⓞR
LⒶ HⓐⓗN-DⒺⒺ-Kⓐⓗ-PⒶ

CHECKING OUT

The bill, please.

Voulez-vous me préparer la note, s'il vous plaît.

V(oo)-L(A) V(oo) M(uh) PR(A)-P(ah)-R(A) L(ah) N(O)T SVP

Is this bill correct?

Il y a une erreur dans la note?

(EE)L (EE) (ah) (ew)N (ĕ)R-(ou)R D(ah)ñ L(ah) N(O)T

Do you accept credit cards?

Acceptez-vous les cartes de crédit?

(ah)-S(ĕ)P-T(A) V(oo) L(A) K(ah)RT D(uh) KR(A)-D(EE)

Could you have my luggage brought down?

Pouvez-vous faire descendre mes bagages?

P(oo)-V(A)-V(oo) F(ĕ)R D(A)-S(ah)ñ-DR(uh) M(A) B(ah)-G(ah)ZH

Can you call a taxi for me?

Appelez-moi un taxi, s'il vous plaît.

ⓐⓗ-PLⒶ MWⓐⓗ ⓤⓗñ TⓐⓗK-SⒺⒺ SVP

I had a very good time!

Je me suis bien amusé!

ZHⓤⓗ Mⓤⓗ SWⒺⒺ BⒺⒺ-ăñ
N̲ⓐⓗ-Mⓔⓦ-ZⒶ

Thanks for everything.

Merci pour tout.

MĕR-SⒺⒺ PⓞⓞR Tⓞⓞ

I'll see you next time.

A la prochaine.

ⓐⓗ Lⓐⓗ PRⓄ-SHăN

Good-bye

Au revoir

Ⓞ Rⓤⓗ-VWⓐⓗR

RESTAURANT SURVIVAL

From sidewalk cafés to the most elegant restaurants, you will find a delectable assortment of French cuisine. Bon appetit!

- Breakfast, **le petit déjeuner**, is usually small and served at your hotel. Lunch, **le déjeuner**, is normally served from 12:30 PM to 3 PM. Dinner, **le dîner**, begins after 7 PM and can extend for hours. It is more formal than lunch and a time for enjoyment of great French cuisine and wine!
- You will find menus posted outside eating establishments and they may contain the following statements: (**Service Compris**) service included or (**Non Compris**) service not included. Most restaurants include tax and a service charge.
- Some restaurants may charge for meals by **"prix-fixe,"** a set menu usually including two or three courses for one set price or **"a la carte."**
- Café prices will be more expensive in high tourist areas. Prices can vary by counter or table seating.

KEY WORDS

Breakfast

le petit déjeuner

Lunch

le déjeuner

Dinner

le dîner

Waiter

Monsieur

M(uh)-SY(ou)

Waitress

Mademoiselle

M(ah)D-MW(ah)-Z(ĕ)L

Restaurant

le restaurant

L(uh) R(ĕ)S-T(O)-R(ah)ñ

USEFUL PHRASES

A table for...

Une table à...

(ew)N T(ah)B-L(uh) (ah)...

2	**4**	**6**
deux	quatre	six
D(ou)	K(ah)-TR(uh)	S(EE)S

The menu, please.

La carte, s'il vous plaît.

L(ah) K(ah)RT SVP

Separate checks, please.

L'addition individuelle, s'il vous plaît.

L(ah)-D(EE)-S(EE)-(O)ñ
(ă)ñ-D(EE)-V(EE)-J(oo)-(ĕ)L SVP

We are in a hurry.

Nous sommes pressés.

N(oo) S(O)M PR(ĕ)-S(A)

What do you recommend?

Qu'est-ce que vous recommandez?

K(ĕ)S K(uh) V(oo) R(uh)-K(O)-M(ah)ñ-D(A)

Please bring me...

Apportez-moi...s'il vous plaît.

ⓐⓗ-P⓪R-TⒶ MWⓐⓗ... SVP

Please bring us...

Apportez-nous...

ⓐⓗ-P⓪R-TⒶ N⓪⓪... SVP

I'm hungry.

J'ai faim.

ZHⒶ Fⓐñ

I'm thirsty.

J'ai soif.

ZHⒶ SWⓐⓗF

Is service included?

Le service est compris?

Lⓤⓗ SⓔR-VⒺⒺS Ⓐ K⓪ñ-PRⒺⒺ

The bill, please.

L'addition, s'il vous plaît.

Lⓐⓗ-DⒺⒺ-SⒺⒺ-⓪ñ SVP

PHRASEMAKER

Ordering beverages is easy and a great way to practice your French! In many foreign countries you will have to request ice with your drinks.

Please bring me...

Apportez-moi...

ⓐⓗ-PⓄR-TⒶ MWⓐⓗ... SVP

▸ **coffee**

du café

Dⓔⓦ Kⓐⓗ-FⒶ

▸ **tea**

du thé

Dⓔⓦ TⒶ

▸ **with cream**

avec de la crème

ⓐⓗ-VⓔK Dⓤⓗ Lⓐⓗ KRⓔM

▸ **with sugar**

avec du sucre

ⓐⓗ-VⓔK Dⓔⓦ Sⓔⓦ-KRⓤⓗ

▸ **with lemon**

avec du citron

ⓐⓗ-VⓔK Dⓔⓦ SⒺⒺ-TRⓄñ

▸ **with ice**

avec de la glace

ⓐⓗ-VⓔK Dⓤⓗ Lⓐⓗ GLⓐⓗS

Soft drinks

Les sodas

LⒶ SⓄ-D(ah)

Milk

Le lait

Hot chocolate

Le chocolat chaud

Juice

Le jus

L(uh) ZH(ew)

Orange juice

Le jus d'orange

Ice water

L'eau glacée

LⓄ GL(ah)-SⒶ

Mineral water

L'eau minérale

LⓄ M(EE)-NⒶ-R(ah)L

AT THE BAR

Bartender

Le bar man

L(uh) B(ah)R M(ah)N

The wine list

La carte des vins

L(ah) K(ah)RT D(A) V(ă)ñ

Cocktail

Le cocktail

L(uh) K(ah)K-T(A)L

On the rocks

Aux glaçons

(O) GL(ah)-S(O)ñ

Straight

Sans glaçons

S(ah)ñ GL(ah)-S(O)ñ

With lemon

Avec du citron

(ah)-V(ĕ)K D(ew) S(EE)-TR(O)ñ

PHRASEMAKER

I would like a glass of...

Je voudrais un verre...

ZH(uh) V(oo)-DR(A) (uh)ñ V(ĕ)R...

▸ **champagne**

de champagne

D(uh) SH(ah)ñ-P(ah)ñ-Y(uh)

▸ **beer**

de bière

D(uh) B(EE)-(ĕ)R

▸ **wine**

de vin

D(uh) V(ă)ñ

▸ **red wine**

de vin rouge

D(uh) V(ă)ñ R(oo)ZH

▸ **white wine**

de vin blanc

D(uh) V(ă)ñ BL(ah)ñ

ORDERING BREAKFAST

In France **"le petit déjeuner"** (breakfast) is usually small, consisting of a croissant or French bread with butter and jam and accompanied by café au lait, hot tea, or hot chocolate.

Bread

Le pain

L(uh) P(ă)ñ

Toast

Le toast

L(uh) T(O)ST

---

with butter

avec du beurre

(ah)-V(ĕ)K D(ew) B(ou)R

---

with jam

avec de la confiture

(ah)-V(ĕ)K D(uh) L(ah) K(O)ñ-F(EE)-T(ew)R

Cereal

Les céréales

L(A) S(A)-R(A)-(ah)L

PHRASEMAKER

I would like...

Je voudrais...

ZH(uh) V(oo)-DR(A)...

▸ **two eggs...**

deux oeufs...

D(ou) Z(ou)...

▸ **scrambled**

brouillés

BR(oo)-Y(A)

▸ **fried**

sur le plat

S(ew)R L(uh) PL(ah)

▸ **with bacon**

avec du bacon

(ah)-V(ĕ)K D(ew) B(ah)-K(O)ñ

▸ **with ham**

avec du jambon

(ah)-V(ĕ)K D(ew) ZH(ah)M-B(O)ñ

▸ **with potatoes**

avec des pommes de terre

(ah)-V(ĕ)K D(A) P(uh)M D(uh) T(ĕ)R

LUNCH AND DINNER

Although you are encouraged to sample great French cuisine, it is important to be able to order foods you are familiar with. This section will provide words and phrases to help you.

I would like...

Je voudrais...

ZH(uh) V(oo)-DR(A)...

We would like...

Nous voudrions...

N(oo) V(oo)-DR(EE)-(O)ñ...

Bring us...

Apportez-nous...

(ah)-P(O)R-T(A) N(oo)... SVP

The lady would like...

La madame voudrait...

L(ah) M(ah)-D(ah)M V(oo)-DR(A)...

The gentleman would like...

Le monsieur voudrait...

L(uh) M(uh)-SY(ou) V(oo)-DR(A)...

STARTERS

Appetizers

Les hors d'oeuvres

LⒶ Z̲ⓄR-D(ou)-VR(uh)

Bread and butter

Le pain et le beurre

L(uh) P(ă)ñ Ⓐ L(uh) B(ou)R

Cheese

Le fromage

L(uh) FRⓄ-M(ah)ZH

Fruit

Le fruit

L(uh) FRW(EE)

Salad

La salade

L(ah) S(ah)-L(ah)D

Soup

La soupe

L(ah) S(oo)P

MEATS

Bacon

Le bacon

Beef

Le boeuf

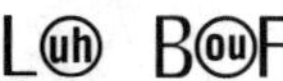

Beef steak

Le bifteck

Ham

Le jambon

Lamb

L'agneau

L(ah)-NY(O)

Pork

Le porc

Veal

Le veau

L(uh) V(O)

POULTRY

Baked chicken

Le poulet au four

L(uh) P(oo)-L(A) (O) F(oo)R

Broiled chicken

Le poulet grillé

L(uh) P(oo)-L(A) GR(EE)-Y(A)

Fried chicken

Le poulet frit

L(uh) P(oo)-L(A) FR(EE)

Duck

Le canard

L(uh) K(ah)-N(ah)R

Goose

L'oie

LW(ah)

Turkey

La dinde

L(ah) D(ă)ñD

SEAFOOD

Fish

Le poisson

Lobster

L'homard

L(O)-M(ah)R

Oysters

Les huîtres

Salmon

Le saumon

Shrimp

La crevette

Trout

La truite

Tuna

Le thon

L(uh) T(O)ñ

OTHER ENTREES

Sandwich

Le sandwich

L(uh) S(ah)ñ-W(EE)SH

Hot dog

Le hot-dog

L(uh) H(ah)T D(ah)G

Hamburger

Le hamburger

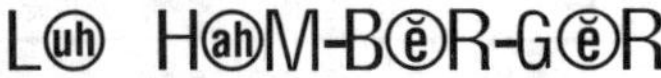
L(uh) H(ah)M-B(ĕ)R-G(ĕ)R

French fries

Les frites

L(A) FR(EE)T

Pasta

Les pâtes

L(A) P(ah)T

Pizza

La pizza

L(ah) P(EE)D-Z(ah)

VEGETABLES

Carrots

Les carottes

L(A) K(ah)-R(O)T

Corn

Le maïs

L(uh) M(ah)-(EE)S

Mushrooms

Les champignons

L(A) SH(ah)ñ-P(EE)-NY(O)ñ

Onions

Les oignons

L(A) Z(O)-NY(O)ñ

Potato

La pomme de terre

L(ah) P(uh)M D(uh) T(ĕ)R

Rice

Le riz

L(uh) R(EE)

Tomato

La tomate

L(ah) T(O)-M(ah)T

FRUITS

Apple

La pomme

Banana

La banane

Grapes

Les raisins

L(A) R(A)-Z(ă)ñ

Lemon

Le citron

Orange

L'orange

L(O)-R(ah)ñZH

Strawberry

La fraise

L(ah) FR(ĕ)Z

Watermelon

La pastèque

L(ah) P(ah)S-T(ĕ)K

DESSERT

Desserts

Les desserts

L(A) D(A)-S(ĕ)R

Apple pie

La tarte aux pommes

L(ah) T(ah)RT (O) P(uh)M

Cherry pie

La tarte aux cerises

L(ah) T(ah)RT (O) S(ĕ)-R(EE)S

Pastries

Les pâtisseries

L(A) P(ah)-T(EE)-S(ĕ)-R(EE)

Candy

Les bonbons

L(A) B(O)ñ B(O)ñ

Ice cream

La glace

L(ah) GL(ah)S

Ice-cream cone

La cone

L(ah) K(O)N

Chocolate

Au chocolat

(O) SH(O)-K(O)-L(ah)

Strawberry

A la fraise

(ah) L(ah) FR(ĕ)Z

Vanilla

A la vanille

(ah) L(ah) V(ah)-N(EE)

CONDIMENTS

Butter

Le beurre

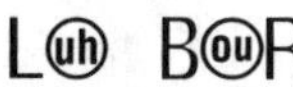

Ketchup

Le ketchup

Mayonnaise

La mayonnaise

Lah MA-YO-NĕZ

Mustard

La moutarde

Lah Moo-TahRD

Salt

Le sel

Luh SĕL

Pepper

Le poivre

Luh PWah-VRuh

Sugar

Le sucre

Luh Sew-KRuh

Vinegar and oil

La vinaigrette

Lah VEE-NA-GRĕT

SETTINGS

A cup

Une tasse

ⓔⓦN T ⓐⓗS

A glass

Un verre

ⓤⓗñ VⓔR

A spoon

Une cuillère

ⓔⓦN KWⒺⒺ-ⓔR

A fork

Une fourchette

ⓔⓦN FⓞⓞR-SHⓔT

A knife

Un couteau

ⓤⓗñ Kⓞⓞ-TⓄ

A plate

Une assiette

ⓔⓦN Nⓐⓗ-SⒺⒺ-ⓔT

A napkin

Une serviette

ⓔⓦN SⓔR-VⒺⒺ-ⓔT

HOW DO YOU WANT IT COOKED?

Baked

Cuit au four

KWⓔⓔT Ⓞ FⓞⓞR

Broiled

Grillé

GRⓔⓔ-YⒶ

Steamed

A l'étuvée

ⓐⓗ LⒶ-Tⓔⓦ-VⒶ

Fried

Frit

FRWⓔⓔ

Rare

Saignant

SⒶ-NYⓐⓗñ

Medium

A point

ⓐⓗ PWⓐⓗñ

Well done

Bien cuit

Bⓔⓔ-ⓐ̆ñ KWⓔⓔ

PROBLEMS

I didn't order this.

Je n'ai pas commandé ceci.

ZH(uh) N(A) P(ah) K(O)-M(ah)N-D(A) S(uh)-S(EE)

Is the bill correct?

Il y a une erreur dans la note?

(EE)L (EE) (ah) (ew)N (ĕ)R-R(ou)R

D(ah)ñ L(ah) N(O)T

Please bring me.

Apportez moi...s'il vous plaît.

(ah)-P(O)R-T(A) MW(ah)... SVP

GETTING AROUND

Getting around in a foreign country can be an adventure in itself! Taxi and bus drivers do not always speak English, so it is essential to be able to give simple directions. The words and phrases in this chapter will help you get where you're going.

- The best way to get a taxi is to ask your hotel or restaurant to call one for you or go to the nearest taxi stand, **"Stationnement de Taxi."** Tipping is customary.

- Trains are used frequently by visitors to Europe. They are efficient and provide connections between large cities and towns throughout the country. Arrive early to allow time for ticket purchasing and checking in, and remember, trains leave on time!

- **Le Métro** or subway is an inexpensive underground train system in Paris. It is easily accessible and a great way to get around. "**M**" signifies a metro stop!

- Check with your travel agent about special rail passes which allow unlimited travel within a set period of time.

KEY WORDS

Airport

L' aéroport

L(ah)-(A)-R(O)-P(O)R

Bus Station / Bus Stop

Le gare routière
L'arrêt de bus

L(uh) G(ah)R R(oo)-T(EE)-(ĕ)R
L(ah)-R(ĕ) D(uh) B(ew)S

Car Rental Agency

L'agence de location

L(ah)-ZH(ah)ñS D(uh) L(O)-K(ah)-S(EE)-(O)ñ

Subway Station

Le métro

L(uh) M(A)-TR(O)

Taxi Stand

La station de taxis

L(ah) ST(ah)-S(EE)-(O)ñ D(uh) T(ah)K-S(EE)

Train Station

La gare

L(ah) G(ah)R

AIR TRAVEL

Arrivals
Les arrivées
LⒶ Z̲(ah)-R(EE)-VⒶ

Departures
Les départs
LⒶ DⒶ-P(ah)R

Flight number
Le vol numéro
L(uh) VⓄL N(ew)-MⒶ-RⓄ

Airline
La ligne aérienne
L(ah) L(EE)N-Y(uh) (ah)-Ⓐ-R(EE)-(ĕ)N

The gate
La porte
L(ah) PⓄRT

Information
Les renseignements
LⒶ R(ah)ñ-S(ĕ)N-Y(uh)-M(ah)ñ

Ticket (airline)
Le billet
L(uh) B(EE)-YⒶ

Reservations
Les réservations
LⒶ RⒶ-S(ĕ)R-V(ah)-S(EE)-Ⓞñ

PHRASEMAKER

I would like a seat...
Je voudrais une place...
ZH(uh) V(oo)-DR(A) (ew)N PL(ah)S...

- **in first class**
  à première classe
  (ah) PR(uh)M-Y(ĕ)R KL(ah)S

- **in the no-smoking section**
  dans la zone non fumeurs
  D(ah)ñ L(ah) Z(O)N N(O)ñ F(ew)-M(ou)R

- **next to the window**
  à côté de la fenêtre
  (ah) K(O)-T(A) D(uh) L(ah)
  F(uh)-N(ĕ)-TR(uh)

- **on the aisle**
  au couloir
  (O) K(oo)L-W(ah)R

- **near the exit**
  près de la sortie
  PR(A) D(uh) L(ah) S(O)R-T(EE)

BY BUS

Bus

L'autobus

LⓄ-TⓄ-B(ew)S

Where is the bus stop?

Où est l'arrêt d'autobus?

(oo) Ⓐ L(ah)-R(ĕ) DⓄ-TⓄ-B(ew)S

Do you go to...?

Vous allez à...?

V(oo) Z(ah)-LⒶ (ah)...

What is the fare?

C'est combien?

SⒶ KⓄñ-B(EE)-(ă)ñ

Do I need exact change?

Est-ce que j'ai besoin de monnaie précise?

(ĕ)S-K(uh) ZHⒶ B(uh)-ZW(ă)ñ D(uh) MⓄ-NⒶ PRⒶ-S(EE)S

How often do the buses run?

Les autobus sont tous les combien?

LⒶ ZⓄ-TⓄ-B(ew)S SⓄñ T(oo) LⒶ KⓄñ-B(EE)-(ă)ñ

PHRASEMAKER

Please tell me...

Dites-moi...s'il vous plaît

D(EE)T MW(ah)... SVP

- **which bus goes to...**

  quel autobus va à...

  K(ĕ) L(O)-T(O)-B(ew)S V(ah) (ah)...

- **what time the bus leaves**

  à quelle heure est-ce que, l'autobus départ

  (ah) K(ĕ) L(ou)R (ĕ)S-K(uh)
  L(O)-T(O)-B(ew)S D(A)-P(ah)R

- **where the bus stop is**

  où est l'arrêt d'autobus

  (oo) (A) L(ah)-R(ĕ) D(O)-T(O)-B(ew)S

- **where to get off**

  où est-ce qu'il faut descendre

  (oo) (ĕ)S-K(EE)L F(O) D(A)-S(ah)ñ-DR(uh)

BY CAR

Fill it up.

Faites le plein.

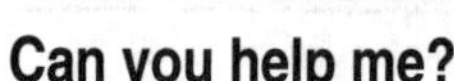

F(ĕ)T L(uh) PL(ă)ñ

Can you help me?

Vous pouvez m'aider?

V(oo) P(oo)-V(A) M(A)-D(A)

My car won't start.

Ma voiture ne démarre pas.

M(ah) VW(ah)-T(ew)R N(uh) D(A)-M(ah)R P(ah)

Can you fix it?

Vous pouvez la réparer?

V(oo) P(oo)-V(A) L(ah) R(A)-P(ah)-R(A)

What will it cost?

Combien est-ce que cela coûte?

K(O)ñ-B(EE)-(ă)ñ (ĕ)S-K(uh) S(uh)-L(ah) K(oo)T

How long will it take?

Ça va prendre combien de temps?

S(ah) V(ah) PR(ah)ñ-DR(uh) K(O)ñ-B(EE)-(ă)ñ D(uh) T(ah)ñ

PHRASEMAKER

Please check...

Vérifiez...s'il vous plaît

VⒶ-RⒺⒺ-FYⒶ.... SVP

- **the battery**

  la batterie

  L(ah) B(ah)-T(ĕ)-R(EE)

- **the brakes**

  les freins

  LⒶ FR(ĕ)N

- **the oil**

  l'huile

  L(ew)-(EE)L

- **the tires**

  les pneus

  LⒶ P(uh)-N(ou)

- **the water**

  l'eau

  LⓄ

SUBWAYS AND TRAINS

Where is the subway station?

Où est le métro?

(oo) (A) L(uh) M(A)-TR(O)

Where is the train station?

Où est la gare?

(oo) (A) L(ah) G(ah)R

A one-way ticket, please.

Un aller, s'il vous plaît.

(uh)ñ N(ah)-L(A) svp

A round trip ticket.

Un aller et retour.

(uh)ñ N(ah)-L(A) (A) R(uh)-T(oo)R

First class

Première classe

PR(uh)M-Y(ĕ)R KL(ah)S

Second class

Deuxième classe

D(ou)-Z(EE)-(ĕ)M KL(ah)S

Which train do I take to go to...?

Quel train est-ce que je prends pour aller à...?

K(ĕ)L TR(ă)ñ (ĕ)S-K(uh) ZH(uh) PR(ah)ñ P(oo)R (ah)-L(A) (ah)...

What is the fare?

C'est combien?

S(A) K(O)ñ-B(EE)-(ă)ñ

Is this seat taken?

La place est libre?

L(ah) PL(ah)S (A) L(EE)-BR(uh)

Do I have to change trains?

Est-ce qu'il faut changer de train?

(ĕ)S-K(EE)L F(O) SH(ah)ñ-ZH(A) D(uh) TR(ă)ñ

Does this train stop at...?

Est-ce que ce train s'arrête à...?

(ĕ)S-K(uh) S(uh) TR(ă)ñ S(ah)-R(ĕ) T(ah)...

Where are we?

Où sommes-nous?

(oo) S(O)M N(oo)

BY TAXI

Can you call a taxi for me?

Appelez-moi un taxi, s'il vous plaît.

Are you available?

Vous êtes libre?

V(oo) Z(ĕ)T L(EE)-BR(uh)

I want to go...

Je voudrais aller...

ZH(uh) V(oo)-DR(A) Z(ah)-L(A)...

Stop here, please.

Arrêtez ici, s'il vous plaît.

(ah)-R(ĕ)-T(A) Z(EE)-S(EE) SVP

Please wait.

Attendez, s'il vous plaît.

(ah)-T(ah)ñ-D(A) SVP

How much do I owe?

Combien est-ce que je dois?

K(O)ñ-B(EE)-(ă)ñ (ĕ)S-K(uh) ZH(uh) DW(ah)

PHRASEMAKER

I would like to go...

Je voudrais aller...

ZH(uh) V(oo)-DR(A) <u>Z</u>(ah)-L(A)...

▸ **to this address**

à cet adresse

(ah) S(ĕ)T (ah)-DR(ĕ)S

▸ **to the airport**

à l'aéroport

(ah) L(ah)-(A)-R(O)-P(O)R

▸ **to the bank**

à la banque

(ah) L(ah) B(ah)NK

▸ **to the hotel**

à l'hôtel

(ah) L(O)-T(ĕ)L

▸ **to the hospital**

à l'hôpital

(ah) L(O)-P(EE)-T(ah)L

▸ **to the subway station**

au métro

(O) M(A)-TR(O)

SHOPPING

Whether you plan a major shopping spree or just need to purchase some basic necessities, the following information is useful.

- Palais de Congrès de Paris and Forum des Halles are popular shopping centers in Paris.
- Department stores are open Monday through Saturday between 9:30 AM and 6:00 PM. Smaller stores may close for lunch between noon and 2:00 PM. Outdoor markets are only open for limited hours.
- There are three main flea markets in Paris providing wonderful opportunities to find treasures.
- Always keep receipts for everything you buy!

SIGNS TO LOOK FOR:

BOULANGERIE (Bakery)
BUREAU DE TABAC (Smoke shop, stamps)
CARTES POSTALES (Post cards)
GRAND MAGASIN (Department store)
CHAUSSURES (Shoes)
SUPERMARCHE (Supermarket)

KEY WORDS

Credit card

La carte de crédit

Money

L'argent

Receipt

Le reçu

L(uh) R(uh)-S(ew)

Sale

La vente

L(ah) V(ah)ñT

Store

Le magasin

L(uh) M(ah)-G(ah)-Z(ă)ñ

Travelers' checks

Les chèques de voyage

L(A) SH(ĕ)K D(uh) VW(ah)-Y(ah)ZH

USEFUL PHRASES

Do you sell...?

Est-ce que vous vendez...?

ⓔ̆S-Kⓤⓗ Vⓞⓞ Vⓐⓗñ-DⒶ...

Do you have...?

Avez-vous...?

ⓐⓗ-VⒶ Vⓞⓞ...

I want to buy...

Je voudrais acheter...

ZHⓤⓗ Vⓞⓞ-DRⒶ ⓐⓗSH-TⒶ...

How much?

Combien?

KⓄñ-BⒺⒺ-ⓐ̆ñ

When are the shops open?

Quand est-ce que les boutiques s'ouvrent?

Kⓐⓗñ Tⓔ̆S-Kⓤⓗ LⒶ
Bⓞⓞ-TⒺⒺK Sⓞⓞ-VRⓤⓗ

No, thank you.

Non, merci.

NⓄñ Mⓔ̆R-SⒺⒺ

I´m just looking.

Je regarde seulement.

ZH(uh) R(uh)-G(ah)RD S(ou)L-M(ah)ñ

It's very expensive.

C'est trop cher.

S(A) TR(O) SH(ĕ)R

Can't you give me a discount?

Pouvez-vous me donner un prix réduit?

P(oo)-V(A) V(oo) M(uh) D(O)-N(A) (uh)ñ
PR(EE) R(A)-DW(EE)

I'll take it!

Je le prendrai!

ZH(uh) L(uh) PR(ah)ñ-DR(A)

I'd like a receipt please.

Je voudrais un reçu.

ZH(uh) V(oo)-DR(A) (uh)ñ R(uh)-S(ew)

I want to return this.

Je voudrais rendre ceci.

ZH(uh) V(oo)-DR(A) R(ah)ñ-DR(uh) S(uh)-S(EE)

It doesn't fit.

Ça ne va pas.

S(ah) N(uh) V(ah) P(ah)

PHRASEMAKER

I'm looking for...

Je cherche...

ZH(uh) SH(ĕ)RSH...

▸ **a bakery**

une boulangerie

(ew)N B(oo)-L(ah)ñ-ZH(uh)-R(EE)

▸ **a bank**

une banque

(ew)N B(ah)NK

▸ **a barber shop**

un coiffeur

(uh)ñ KW(ah)-F(ou)R

▸ **a camera shop**

un photo station

(uh)ñ F(O)-T(O) ST(ah)-S(EE)-(O)ñ

▸ **a hair salon**

une coiffure

(ew)N KW(ah)-F(ew)R

▸ **a pharmacy**

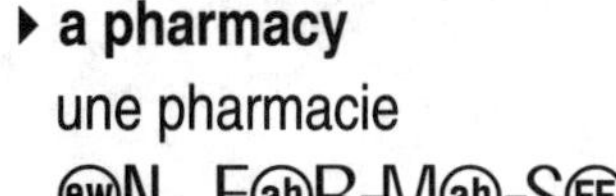

une pharmacie

(ew)N F(ah)R-M(ah)-S(EE)

PHRASEMAKER

Do you sell...

Est-ce que vous vendez...

ĕS-Kuh Voo Vahñ-DA...

- **aspirin?**

  l'aspirine?

  LahS-PEE-REEN

- **cigarettes?**

  les cigarettes?

  LA SEE-Gah-RĕT

- **deodorant?**

  le deodorant?

  Luh DA-O-DO-Rahñ

- **dresses?**

  les robes?

  LA ROB

- **film?**

  la pellicule?

  Lah Pĕ-LEE-KewL

▸ **pantyhose?**

le collant?

L(uh) K(O)-L(ah)ñ

▸ **perfume?**

le parfum?

L(uh) P(ah)R-F(uh)ñ

▸ **razor blades?**

les lames de rasoir?

L(A) L(ah)M D(uh) R(ah)-SW(ah)R

▸ **shampoo?**

le shampooing?

L(uh) SH(ah)M-P(oo)-(EE)N

▸ **shaving cream?**

la crème à raser?

L(ah) KR(ĕ)M (ah) R(ah)-S(A)

▸ **shirts?**

les chemises?

L(A) SH(uh)-M(EE)Z

▸ **soap?**

le savon?

L(uh) S(ah)-V(O)ñ

▸ **sunglasses?**

les lunettes de soleil?

L(A) L(ew)-N(ĕ)T D(uh) S(O)-L(A)

▸ **sunscreen?**

la crème solaire?

L(ah) KR(ĕ)M S(O)-L(ĕ)R

▸ **toothbrushes?**

les brosses à dents?

L(A) BR(O) S(ah) D(ah)ñ

▸ **toothpaste?**

le dentifrice?

L(uh) D(ah)ñ-T(EE)-FR(EE)S

▸ **water? (bottled)**

l'eau nature?

L(O) N(ah)-T(ew)R

▸ **water? (mineral)**

l'eau minérale?

L(O) M(EE)-N(A)-R(ah)L

ESSENTIAL SERVICES

THE BANK

As a traveler in a foreign country your primary contact with banks will be to exchange money. Keep in mind that many banks close on Monday and Saturday afternoon.

- The French national currency is the Euro (formerly French franc). Bank notes are in denominations of Euro 500, 200, 100, 50, 20, 10 and 5. Coins are in denominations of 2 and 1 euro, and 50, 20, 10, 5, 2, and 1 euro cents.

- Change enough funds before leaving home to pay for tips, food, and transportation to your final destination.

- Generally, you will receive a better rate of exchange at a bank than at a Bureaux de Change or at the airport.

- Current exchange rates are posted in banks and published daily in city newspapers.

- ATM machines are readily available in large cities like Paris as well as smaller towns, and credit cards are accepted.

KEY WORDS

Bank

La banque

L(ah) B(ah)NK

Exchange office

Le bureau de change

L(uh) B(ew)-R(O) D(uh) SH(ah)ñZH

Money

L'argent

L(ah)R-ZH(ah)ñ

Money order

Le mandat-poste

L(uh) M(ah)ñ-D(ah) P(O)ST

Travelers' checks

Les chèques de voyage

L(A) SH(ĕ)K D(uh) VW(ah)-Y(ah)ZH

USEFUL PHRASES

Where is the bank?

Où est la banque?

ⓞⓞ Ⓐ Lⓐⓗ BⓐⓗNK

What time does the bank open?

A quelle heure est-ce que la banque s'ouvre?

ⓐⓗ Kⓔ̆ L̲ⓞⓤR ⓔ̆S-Kⓤⓗ Lⓐⓗ BⓐⓗNK Sⓞⓞ-VRⓤⓗ

Where is the exchange office?

Où est le bureau de change?

ⓞⓞ Ⓐ Lⓤⓗ Bⓔⓦ-RⓄ Dⓤⓗ SHⓐⓗñZH

What time does the exchange office open?

A quelle heure s'ouvre le bureau de change?

ⓐⓗ Kⓔ̆ L̲ⓞⓤR Sⓞⓞ-VRⓤⓗ Lⓤⓗ Bⓔⓦ-RⓄ Dⓤⓗ SHⓐⓗñZH

Can I change dollars here?

Puis-je changer des dollars ici?

PWⒺⒺ-ZHⓤⓗ SHⓐⓗñ-ZHⒶ DⒶ DⓄ-LⓐⓗR S̲ⒺⒺ-SⒺⒺ

Can you change this?

Pouvez-vous changer ceci?

P⊙⊙-V(A) V⊙⊙ SH(ah)ñ-ZH(A) S(uh)-S(EE)

What is the exchange rate?

Quel est le taux de change?

K(ĕ) L(A) L(uh) T(O) D(uh) SH(ah)ñZH

I would like large bills.

Je voudrais de grands billets.

ZH(uh) V⊙⊙-DR(A) D(uh) GR(ah)ñ B(EE)-Y(A)

I would like small bills.

Je voudrais de petits billets.

ZH(uh) V⊙⊙-DR(A) D(uh) P(uh)-T(EE) B(EE)-Y(A)

I need change.

J'ai besoin de monnaie.

ZH(A) B(uh)-ZW(ă)ñ D(uh) M(O)-N(A)

Do you have an ATM?

Avez-vous un GAB?

(ah)-V(A) V⊙⊙ (uh)ñ ZH(A) (ah) B(A)

POST OFFICE

PTT and **POSTE** identify the post office. Stamps can be purchased at a **Bureau de Tabac**, as well as at certain cafés and in post offices.

KEY WORDS

Airmail

Par avion

P(ah)R (ah)-V(EE)-(O)ñ

Letter

La lettre

L(ah) L(ĕ)-TR(uh)

Post office

La poste

L(ah) P(O)ST

Postcard

La carte postale

L(ah) K(ah)RT P(O)S-T(ah)L

Stamp

Le timbre

L(uh) T(ă)ñ-BR(uh)

USEFUL PHRASES

Where is the post office?

Où est la poste?

ⓞⓞ Ⓐ Lⓐⓗ PⓄST

What time does the post office open?

A quelle heure est-ce que la poste s'ouvre?

ⓐⓗ Kⓔ L̲ⓞⓤR ⓔS-Kⓤⓗ Lⓐⓗ PⓄST Sⓞⓞ-VRⓤⓗ

I need stamps.

J'ai besoin de timbres.

ZHⒶ Bⓤⓗ-ZWⓐñ Dⓤⓗ Tⓐñ-BRⓤⓗ SVP

I need an envelope.

J'ai besoin d'une enveloppe.

ZHⒶ Bⓤⓗ-ZWⓐñ DⓔⓦN ⓐⓗñ-Vⓔ-LⓄP

I need a pen.

J'ai besoin d'un stylo.

ZHⒶ Bⓤⓗ-ZWⓐñ Dⓤⓗñ STⒺⒺ-LⓄ

TELEPHONE

Placing phone calls in a foreign country can be a test of will and stamina! Besides the obvious language barriers, service can vary greatly from one town to the next.

- In France, phone calls can be made from the post office, Métro station and most cafés with phone cards **télécarte.**

- Coin operated booths still exist; however, they are often difficult to find. If you plan to make frequent use of the French phone system, it is best to purchase a **télécarte** as soon as possible.

- You can purchase a telephone card at tobacconists, post offices, and approved sales points which display the poster **TELECARTE EN VENTE ICI.** These cards allow you to easily make calls in most phone booths in France.

KEY WORDS

Information

Les renseignements

L(A) R(ah)ñ-S(ĕ)N-Y(uh)-M(ah)ñ

Long distance

De communication interurbaine

D(uh) K(O)-M(ew)-N(EE)-K(ah)-S(EE)-(O)ñ
(ă)ñ-T(ĕ)R-(ew)R-B(ĕ)N

Operator

Le standardiste

L(uh) ST(ah)N-D(ah)R-D(EE)ST

Phone book

L'annuaire

L(ah)-N(ew)-(ĕ)R

Public telephone

Le téléphone public

L(uh) T(A)-L(A)-F(O)N P(ew)-BL(EE)K

Telephone

Le téléphone

L(uh) T(A)-L(A)-F(O)N

USEFUL PHRASES

May I use your telephone?

Puis-je me servir de votre téléphone?

PW(EE)-ZH(uh) M(uh) S(ĕ)R-V(EE)R D(uh)
V(O)-TR(uh) T(A)-L(A)-F(O)N

Operator, I don't speak French.

Madame (monsieur) le standardiste,
je ne parle pas français.

M(ah)-D(ah)M L(uh) ST(ah)N-D(ah)R-D(EE)ST
ZH(uh)N-(uh) P(ah)RL P(ah) FR(ah)ñ-S(A)

I would like to make a long-distance call.

Je voudrais donner un coup de communication interurbaine.

ZH(uh) V(oo)-DR(A) D(O)-N(A) (uh)ñ K(oo) D(uh)
T(A)-L(A)-F(O)N D(uh) K(O)-M(ew)-N(EE)-K(ah)-S(EE)-(O)ñ
(ă)ñ-T(ĕ)R-(ew)R-B(ĕ)N

I would like to make a call to the United States.

Je voudrais donner un coup de téléphone aux Etats-Unis.

ZH(uh) V(oo)-DR(A) D(O)-N(A) (uh)ñ K(oo) D(uh)
T(A)-L(A)-F(O)N (O) Z(A)-T(ah)-Z(ew)-N(EE)

I want to call...

Je voudrais téléphoner...

ZH(uh) V(oo)-DR(A) T(A)-L(A)-F(O)-N(A)...

SIGHTSEEING AND ENTERTAINMENT

In most towns in France you will find tourist information offices. Here you can usually obtain brochures, maps, historical information, bus and train schedules.

Lively places, an abundance of atmosphere, shopping, festivals, great food, and fine wine invite travelers to experience all that France has to offer.

PARIS SIGHTS

L'Arc de Triomphe
L(ah)RK D(uh) TR(EE)-(O)ñF

Le Louvre
L(uh) L(oo)-VR(uh)

La Tour Eiffel
L(ah) T(oo)R (EE)-F(ĕ)L

Notre Dame
N(O)-TR(uh) D(ah)M

Les Champs-Elysées
L(A) SH(ah)ñ-Z(A)-L(EE)-S(A)

KEY WORDS

Admission

L'entrée

L(ah)ñ-TR(A)

Map

Le plan

L(uh) PL(ah)ñ

Reservation

La réservation

L(ah) R(A)-S(ĕ)R-V(ah)-S(EE)-(O)ñ

Ticket

Le ticket

L(uh) T(EE)-K(A)

Tour

La visite

L(ah) V(EE)-Z(EE)T

Tour guide

Le guide

L(uh) G(EE)D

USEFUL PHRASES

Where is the tourist office?

Où est le Syndicat d'Initiative?

ⓞⓞ Ⓐ Lⓤⓗ Sⓐñ-DⒺⒺ-Kⓐⓗ DⒺⒺ-NⒺⒺ-SⒺⒺ-ⓐⓗ-TⒺⒺV

Is there a tour to...?

Y a-t-il une visite guidée à...?

ⒺⒺ ⓐⓗ-TⒺⒺL ⓔⓦN VⒺⒺ-ZⒺⒺT GⒺⒺ-DⒶ ⓐⓗ...

Where do I buy a ticket?

Où puis-je acheter un ticket?

ⓞⓞ PWⒺⒺ-ZHⓤⓗ ⓐⓗSH-TⒶ ⓤⓗñ TⒺⒺ-KⒶ

How much does the tour cost?

Combien coûte la visite?

KⓄñ-BⒺⒺ-ⓐñ KⓞⓞT Lⓐⓗ VⒺⒺ-ZⒺⒺT

How long does the tour take?

La visite prend combien de temps?

Lⓐⓗ VⒺⒺ-ZⒺⒺT PRⓐⓗñ KⓄñ-BⒺⒺ-ⓐñ Dⓤⓗ Tⓐⓗñ

Does the guide speak English?

Est-ce que le guide parle anglais?

(ĕ)S-K(uh) L(uh) G(EE)D P(ah)RL (ah)ñ-GL(A)

Are children free?

Y a-t-il un tarif pour enfants?

(EE) (ah)-T(EE)L (uh)ñ T(ah)-R(EE)F P(oo)R (ah)ñ-F(ah)ñ

What time does the show start?

A quelle heure commence le spectacle?

(ah) K(ĕ) L(ou)R K(O)-M(ah)ñS L(uh) SP(ĕ)K-T(ah)-KL(uh)

Do I need reservations?

Il faut avoir des réservations?

(EE)L F(O) T(ah)-VW(ah)R D(A) R(A)-S(ĕ)R-V(ah)-S(EE)-(O)ñ

Where can we go dancing?

Où est-ce qu'on peut danser?

(oo) (ĕ)S K(O)ñ P(ou) D(ah)ñ-S(A)

Is there a minimum cover charge?

Y a-t-il un prix d'entrée?

(EE) (ah)-T(EE)L (uh)ñ PR(EE) D(ah)ñ-TR(A)

PHRASEMAKER

May I invite you...

Je vous invite...

ZH(uh) V(oo) Z(ă)ñ-V(EE)T...

▸ **to a concert?**

à un concert?

(ah) (uh)ñ K(O)ñ-S(ĕ)R

▸ **to dance?**

à danser?

(ah) D(ah)ñ-S(A)

▸ **to dinner?**

au dîner?

(O) D(EE)-N(A)

▸ **to the movies?**

au cinéma?

(O) S(EE)-N(A)-M(ah)

▸ **to the theater?**

au théâtre?

(O) T(A)-(ah)-TR(uh)

PHRASEMAKER

Where can I find...

Où se trouve...

Ⓞ S(uh) TR(oo)V...

▸ **a health club?**

un centre sportif?

(uh)ñ S(ah)ñ-TR(uh) SP(O)R-T(EE)F

▸ **a swimming pool?**

une piscine?

(ew)N P(EE)-S(EE)N

▸ **a tennis court?**

un terrain de tennis?

(uh)ñ T(ĕ)-R(ă)ñ D(uh) T(ĕ)-N(EE)S

▸ **a golf course?**

un terrain de golf?

(uh)ñ T(ĕ)-R(ă)ñ D(uh) G(O)LF

HEALTH

Hopefully you will not need medical attention on your trip. If you do, it is important to communicate basic information regarding your condition.

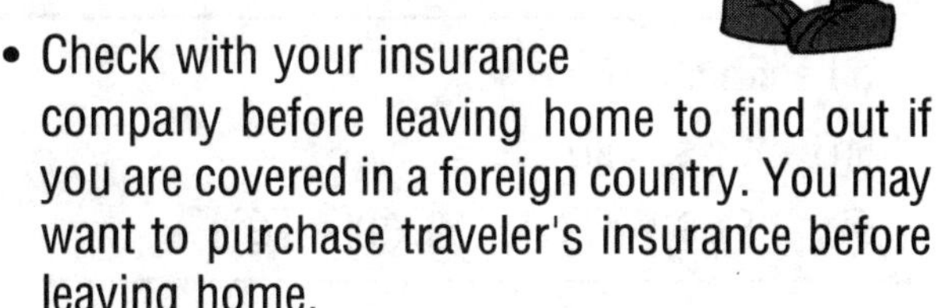

- Check with your insurance company before leaving home to find out if you are covered in a foreign country. You may want to purchase traveler's insurance before leaving home.
- If you take prescription medicine, carry your prescription with you. Have your prescriptions translated before you leave home.
- Take a small first-aid kit with you.
- Your embassy or consulate should be able to assist you in finding health care.
- A **GREEN CROSS** indicates pharmacy, where minor treatment can be handled by the pharmacist. A list of local pharmacies, open at night, is posted in the shop.
- **Droguerie** is similar to a drugstore but also sells household goods and toiletries.
- (H) Indicates Hospital (**L'hôpital**)

KEY WORDS

Ambulance

L'ambulance

L(ah)ñ-B(ew)-L(ah)ñS

Dentist

Le dentiste

L(uh) D(ah)ñ-T(EE)ST

Doctor

Le médecin

L(uh) M(A)-D(uh)-S(ă)ñ

Emergency

L'urgence

L(ew)R-ZH(ah)ñS

Hospital

L'hôpital

L(O)-P(EE)-T(ah)L

Prescription

La prescription

L(ah) PR(ĕ)-SKR(EE)P-S(EE)-(O)ñ

USEFUL PHRASES

I am sick.

Je suis malade.

ZH(uh) SW(EE) M(ah)-L(ah)D

I need a doctor.

J'ai besoin d'un docteur.

ZH(A) B(uh)-ZW(ă)ñ D(uh)ñ D(ah)K-T(ou)R

It's an emergency!

C'est une urgence!

S(A) T(ew) N(ew)R-ZH(ah)ñS

Where is the nearest hospital?

Où est l'hôpital le plus proche?

(oo) (A) L(O)-P(EE)-T(ah)L L(uh) PL(ew) PR(O)SH

Call an ambulance!

Faites venir une ambulance!

F(ĕ)T V(uh)-N(EE)R (ew) N(ah)ñ-B(ew)-L(ah)ñS

I'm allergic to...

Je suis allergique à...

ZH(uh) SW(EE) Z(ah)-L(ĕ)R-ZH(EE) K(ah)...

I'm pregnant.

Je suis enceinte.

ZH(uh) SW(EE) Z(ah)ñ-S(ă)ñT

I'm diabetic.

Je suis diabétique.

ZH(uh) SW(EE) D(EE)-(ah)-B(A)-T(EE)K

I have a heart condition.

Je suis cardiaque.

ZH(uh) SW(EE) K(ah)R-D(EE)-(ah)-K(uh)

I have high blood pressure.

Je fais de l'hypertension.

ZH(uh) F(A) D(uh) L(EE)-P(ĕ)R-T(ah)ñ-S(EE)-(O)ñ

I have low blood pressure.

Je fais de l'hypotension.

ZH(uh) F(A) D(uh) L(EE)-P(O)-T(ah)ñ-S(EE)-(O)ñ

PHRASEMAKER

I need…

J'ai besoin...

ZHⒶ B(uh)-ZW(ă)ñ...

- **a doctor**

  d'un docteur

  D(uh)ñ D(ah)K-T(ou)R

- **a dentist**

  d'un dentiste

  D(uh)ñ D(ah)ñ-T(EE)ST

- **a nurse**

  d'une infirmière

  D(ew) N(ă)ñ-F(EE)R-M(EE)-(ĕ)R

- **an optician**

  d'un opticien

  D(uh)ñ N(O)P-T(EE)-S(EE)-(ă)ñ

- **a pharmacist**

  d'un pharmacien

  D(uh)ñ F(ah)R-M(ah)-S(EE)-(ă)ñ

PHRASEMAKER

(AT THE PHARMACY)

Do you have...

Avez-vous..

(ah)-V(A) V(oo)...

▸ **aspirin?**

l'aspirine?

L(ah)S-P(EE)-R(EE)N

▸ **Band-Aids?**

des bandages?

D(A) B(ah)ñ-D(ah)ZH

▸ **cough medicine?**

le sirop contre la toux?

L(uh) S(EE)-R(O) K(O)ñ-TR(uh) L(ah) T(oo)

▸ **ear drops?**

les gouttes pour les oreilles?

L(A) G(oo)T P(oo)R L(A) Z(O)-R(A)-Y(ou)

▸ **eyedrops?**

les gouttes pour les yeux?

L(A) G(oo)T P(oo)R L(A) Z(EE)-Y(ou)

BUSINESS TRAVEL

It is important to show appreciation and interest in another person's language and culture, particularly when doing business. A few well-pronounced phrases can make a great impression.

I have an appointment.
J'ai rendez-vous.
ZH(A) R(ah)ñ-D(A)-V(oo)

Here is my card.
Voici ma carte.
VW(ah)-S(EE) M(ah) K(ah)RT

May I speak to Mr...?
Puis-je parler à Monsieur...?
PW(EE)-ZH(uh) P(ah)R-L(A) (ah) M(uh)-SY(ou)...

May I speak to Mrs...?
Puis-je parler à Madame...?
PW(EE)-ZH(uh) P(ah)R-L(A) (ah) M(ah)-D(ah)M...

I need an interpreter.
J'ai besoin d'un interprète.
ZH(A) B(uh)-ZW(ă)ñ D(uh)ñ
N(ă)ñ-T(ĕ)R-PR(ĕ)T

KEY WORDS

Appointment

Le rendez-vous

L(uh) R(ah)ñ-D(A)-V(oo)

Meeting

La réunion

L(ah) R(A)-(ew)N-Y(O)ñ

Marketing

Le marketing

L(uh) M(ah)R-K(ĕ)-T(EE)N

Presentation

La présentation

L(ah) PR(A)-S(ĕ)N-T(ah)-S(EE)-(O)ñ

Sales

Les ventes

L(A) V(ah)ñT

PHRASEMAKER

I need...

J'ai besoin...

ZHⒶ B(uh)-ZW(ă)ñ...

- **a computer**

  d'un ordinateur

  D(uh)ñ NⓄR-D(EE)-N(ah)-T(ou)R

- **a copy machine**

  d'un copieur

  D(uh)ñ KⓄ-P(EE)-(ou)R

- **a conference room**

  d'une salle de conférences

  D(ew)N S(ah)L D(uh) KⓄñ-FⒶ-R(ah)ñS

- **a fax machine**

  d'un télécopieur

  D(uh)ñ TⒶ-LⒶ-KⓄ-P(EE)-(ou)R

- **an interpreter**

  d'un interprète

  D(uh)ñ N(ă)ñ-T(ĕ)R-PR(ĕ)T

▸ **a lawyer**

d'un avocat

D(uh)ñ N(ah)-V(O)-K(ah)

▸ **a notary**

d'un notaire

D(uh)ñ N(O)-T(ĕ)R

▸ **overnight delivery**

de livraison exprès

D(uh) L(EE)-VR(A)-S(O)ñ (ĕ)KS-PR(ĕ)

▸ **paper**

de papier

D(uh) P(ah)-P(EE)-(A)

▸ **a pen**

d'un stylo

D(uh)ñ ST(EE)-L(O)

▸ **a pencil**

d'un crayon

D(uh)ñ KR(A)-(O)ñ

▸ **a secretary**

d'un secrétaire

D(uh)ñ S(ĕ)-KR(ĕ)-T(ĕ)R

GENERAL INFORMATION

From cool summers in the west to hot summers and very cold winters in central and eastern France, there is something for everyone!

SEASONS

Spring

le printemps

L(uh) PR(ă)ñ-T(ah)ñ

Summer

l'été

L(A)-T(A)

Autumn

l'automne

L(O)-T(uh)ñ

Winter

l'hiver

L(EE)-V(ĕ)R

THE DAYS

Monday
lundi
L(uh)ñ-D(EE)

Tuesday
mardi
M(ah)R-D(EE)

Wednesday
mercredi
M(ĕ)R-KR(uh)-D(EE)

Thursday
jeudi
ZH(ou)-D(EE)

Friday
vendredi
V(ah)ñ-DR(uh)-D(EE)

Saturday
samedi
S(ah)M-D(EE)

Sunday
dimanche
D(EE)-M(ah)ñSH

THE MONTHS

January
janvier
ZH(ah)ñ-V(EE)-(A)

February
février
F(A)-VR(EE)-(A)

March
mars
M(ah)RS

April
avril
(ah)V-R(EE)L

May
mai
M(A)

June
juin
ZH(oo)-(ă)ñ

July
juillet
ZHW(EE)-(A)

August
août
(oo)T

September
septembre
S(ĕ)P-T(ah)ñ-BR(uh)

October
octobre
(O)K-T(O)-BR(uh)

November
novembre
N(O)-V(ah)ñ-BR(uh)

December
décembre
D(A)-S(ah)ñ-BR(uh)

COLORS

Black

Noir (m) Noire (f)

NW(ah)R

White

Blanc (m) Blanche (f)

BL(ah)ñ BL(ah)ñSH

Blue

Bleu (m) Bleue (f)

BL(ou)

Brown

Brun (m) Brune (f)

BR(uh)ñ BR(ew)N

Gray

Gris (m) Grise (f)

GR(EE) GR(EE)S

Gold

Or

(O)R

Orange

Orange

(O)-R(ah)ñZH

Yellow

Jaune

ZH(O)N

Red

Rouge

R(oo)ZH

Green

Vert (m) Verte (f)

V(ĕ)R V(ĕ)RT

Pink

Rose

R(O)Z

Purple

Violet (m) Violette (f)

V(EE)-(O)-L(A) V(EE)-(O)-L(ĕ)T

NUMBERS

0	**1**	**2**
Zéro	Un	Deux
Z(A)-R(O)	(uh)ñ	D(ou)
3	**4**	**5**
Trois	Quatre	Cinq
TRW(ah)	K(ah)-TR(uh)	S(ă)NK
6	**7**	**8**
Six	Sept	Huit
S(EE)S	S(ĕ)T	W(EE)T
9	**10**	**11**
Neuf	Dix	Onze
N(ou)F	D(EE)S	(O)ñZ
12	**13**	**14**
Douze	Treize	Quatorze
D(oo)Z	TR(ĕ)Z	K(ah)-T(O)RZ
15	**16**	**17**
Quinze	Seize	Dix-sept
K(ă)ñZ	S(ĕ)Z	D(EE)-S(ĕ)T
18	**19**	
Dix-huit	Dix-neuf	
D(EE)Z-W(EE)T	D(EE)Z-N(ou)F	

20 Vingt V(ă)ñ	**30** Trente TR(ah)ñT
40 Quarante K(ĕ)-R(ah)ñT	**50** Cinquante S(ă)ñ-K(ah)ñT
60 Soixante SW(ah)-Z̲(ah)ñT	**70** Soixante-dix SW(ah)-Z̲(ah)ñT D(EE)S
80 Quatre-vingt K(ah)-TR(uh) V(ă)ñ	**90** Quatre-vingt-dix K(ah)-TR(uh) V(ă)ñ D(EE)S
100 Cent S(ah)ñ	**1000** Mille M(EE)L
1,000,000 Million M(EE)-L(EE)-(O)ñ	

DICTIONARY

Each English entry is followed by the French word and then the EPLS Vowel Symbol System. French nouns are either masculine or feminine. The French article **le** precedes masculine nouns and **la** precedes feminine nouns in the singular form. **Les** indicates feminine or masculine plural. In some cases, masculine and feminine are indicated by (m) and (f) respectively.

A

a, an un (m) (uh)ñ une (f) (ew)N

a lot beaucoup B(O)-K(oo)

able (to be) pouvoir P(oo)-VW(ah)R

above au dessus (de) (O) D(uh)-S(ew) D(uh)

accident l'accident (m) L(ah)K-S(EE)-D(ah)ñ

accommodation le logement L(uh) L(O)ZH-M(ah)ñ

account le compte L(uh) K(O)ñT

address l'adresse (f) L(ah)-DR(ĕ)S

admission l'entrée (f) L(ah)ñ-TR(A)

afraid (to be) avoir peur (ah)-VW(ah)R P(ou)R

after après (ah)-PR(A)

afternoon l'après-midi (m) L(ah)-PR(A) M(EE)-D(EE)

air conditioning d'air climatisé (m)
DĕR KL(EE)-M(ah)-T(EE)-Z(A)

aircraft l'avion (m) L(ah)-V(EE)-(O)ñ

airline la ligne aérienne L(ah) L(EE)N (ah)-(A)-R(EE)-(ĕ)N

airport l'aéroport (m) L(ah)-(A)-R(O)-P(O)R

aisle couloir K(oo)L-W(ah)R

all tout (m) T(oo) toute (f) T(oo)T

almost presque PR(ĕ)S-K(uh)

alone seul S(ou)L

also aussi (O)-S(EE)

always toujours T(oo)-ZH(oo)R

ambulance l'ambulance (f) L(ah)ñ-B(ew)-L(ah)ñS

American américain (m) (ah)-M(A)-R(EE)-K(ă)ñ
américaine (f) (ah)-M(A)-R(EE)-K(ĕ)ñ

and et (A)

another un autre (uh)ñ N(O)-TR(uh)

anything quelque chose K(ĕ)L-K(uh) SH(O)Z

apartment l'appartement (m) L(ah)-P(ah)R-T(uh)-M(ah)ñ

appetizers les hors-d'oeuvres (m)
L(A) Z(O)R-D(ou)-VR(uh)

apple la pomme L(ah) P(uh)M

appointment le rendez-vous L(uh) R(ah)ñ-D(A)-V(oo)

April avril (ah)-VR(EE)L

arrival l'arrivée (f) L(ah)-R(EE)-V(A)

arrive (to) arriver (ah)-R(EE)-V(A)

ashtray le cendrier L(uh) S(ah)ñ-DR(EE)-(A)

aspirin l'aspirine (f) L(ah)S-P(EE)-R(EE)N

attention l'attention (f) L(ah)-T(ah)ñ-S(EE)-(O)ñ

August août (oo)T

Australia L'Australie (f) L(O)-STR(ah)-L(EE)

Australian L' australien (m) L(O)-STR(ah)-L(EE)(ă)ñ

L'australienne (f) L(O)-STR(ah)-L(EE)(ĕ)ñ

author l'auteur (m) L(O)-T(ou)R

automobile l'automobile (f) L(O)-T(O)-M(O)-B(EE)L

autumn l'automne L(O)-T(uh)ñ

avenue l'avenue L(ah)-V(uh)-N(ew)

awful affreux (m) (ah)-FR(ou)

affreuse (f) (ah)-FR(ou)Z

B

baby le bébé L(uh) B(A)-B(A)

babysitter le garde-bébé L(uh) G(ah)RD B(A)-B(A)

bacon le bacon L(uh) B(ah)-K(o)ñ

bad mauvais (m) M(o)-V(A)

mauvaise (f) M(o)-V(ĕ)Z

bag le sac L(uh) S(ah)K

baggage les bagages (m) L(A) B(ah)-G(ah)ZH

baked au four (o) F(oo)R

bakery la boulangerie L(ah) B(oo)-L(ah)ñ-ZH(uh)-R(EE)

banana la banane L(ah) B(ah)-N(ah)N

bandage le bandage L(uh) B(ah)N-D(ah)ZH

bank la banque L(ah) B(ah)ñK

barbershop le coiffeur L(uh) KW(ah)-F(ou)R

bartender le barman L(uh) B(ah)R M(ah)N

bath la bain L(ah) B(ă)ñ

bathing suit le maillot de bains

L(uh) M(ah)-Y(o) D(uh) B(ă)ñ

bathroom la salle de bains L(ah) S(ah)L D(uh) B(ă)ñ

battery la batterie L(uh) B(ah)-T(uh)-R(EE)

beach la plage L(ah) PL(ah)ZH

beautiful beau (m) B(o) belle (f) B(ĕ)L

beauty shop le salon de beauté

L(uh) S(ah)-L(o)ñ D(uh) B(o)-T(A)

bed le lit L(uh) L(EE)

beef le boeuf L(uh) B(ou)F

beer la bière L(ah) B(EE)-(ĕ)R

bellman le chasseur L(uh) SH(ah)-S(ou)R

belt la ceinture L(ah) S(ă)ñ-T(ou)R

big grand (m) GR(ah)ñ grande (f) GR(ah)ND

bill l'addition (f) L(ah)-D(EE)-S(EE)-(O)ñ

black noir NW(ah)R

blanket la couverture L(ah) K(oo)-V(ĕ)R-T(ou)R

blue bleu BL(ou)

boat le bateau L(uh) B(ah)-T(O)

book le livre L(uh) L(EE)-VR(uh)

bookstore la librairie L(ah) L(EE)-BR(ĕ)-R(EE)

border la frontière L(ah) FR(O)ñ-T(EE)-(ĕ)R

boy le garçon L(uh) G(ah)R-S(O)ñ

bracelet le bracelet L(uh) BR(ah)-S(uh)-L(A)

brake le frein L(uh) FR(ă)ñ

bread le pain L(uh) P(ă)ñ

breakfast le petit déjeuner

L(uh) P(uh)-T(EE) D(A)-ZH(ou)-N(A)

broiled grillé (f) GR(EE)-Y(A)

brother le frère (m) L(uh) FR(ĕ)R

brush la brosse L(ah) BR(O)S

building le bâtiment L(uh) B(ah)-T(EE)-M(ah)ñ

bus l'autobus (m) L(O)-T(O)-B(ew)S

bus station la gare routière L(ah) G(ah)R R(oo)-T(EE)-(ĕ)R

bus stop l'arrêt de bus (m) L(ah)-R(ĕ) D(uh) B(ew)S

business les affaires (f) L(A) Z̲(ah)-F(ĕ)R

butter le beurre L(uh) B(ou)R

buy (to) acheter (ah)SH-T(A)

C

cab le taxi L(uh) T(ah)K-S(EE)

call (to) appeler (ah)-P(uh)-L(A)

camera l'appareil-photo (m) L(ah)-P(ah)-R(A) F(O)-T(O)

Canada Canada K(ah)-N(ah)-D(ah)

Canadian Canadien (m) K(ah)N-(ah)-D(EE)(ă)ñ

Canadienne (f) K(ah)N-(ah)-D(EE)(ĕ)ñ

candy le bonbon L(uh) B(O)ñ-B(O)ñ

car la voiture L(ah) VW(ah)-T(ew)R

carrot la carotte L(ah) K(ah)-R(O)T

castle le château L(uh) SH(ah)-T(O)

cathedral la cathédrale L(ah) K(ah)-T(A)-DR(ah)L

celebration la fête L(ah) F(ĕ)T

center le centre L(uh) S(ah)ñ-TR(uh)

cereal les céréales L(A) S(A)-R(A)-(ah)L

chair la chaise L(ah) SH(ĕ)Z

champagne la champagne L(ah) SH(ah)ñ-P(ah)N-Y(uh)

change (to) changer SH(ah)ñ-ZH(A)

change (exact) la monnaie précise
L(ah) M(O)-N(A) PR(A)-S(EE)S

change (money) la monnaie L(ah) M(O)-N(A)

cheap bon marché B(O)ñ M(ah)R-SH(A)

check (bill in a restaurant) l'addition (f)
L(ah)-D(EE)-S(EE)-(O)ñ

cheers à votre santé (ah)-V(O)-TR(uh) S(ah)ñ-T(A)

cheese le fromage L(uh) FR(O)-M(ah)ZH

chicken le poulet L(uh) P(oo)-L(A)

child l'enfant L(ah)ñ-F(ah)ñ

chocolate (flavor) au chocolat (O) SH(O)-K(O)-L(ah)

church l'église (f) L(A)-GL(EE)Z

cigar le cigare L(uh) S(EE)-G(ah)R

cigarette la cigarette L(ah) S(EE)-G(ah)-R(ĕ)T

city la ville L(ah) V(EE)L

clean propre PR(O)-PR(uh)

close (to) fermer F(ĕ)R-M(A)

closed fermé F(ĕ)R-M(A)

clothes les vêtements (m) L(A) V(ĕ)T-M(ah)ñ

cocktail le cocktail L(uh) K(ah)K-T(A)L

coffee le café L(uh) K(ah)-F(A)

cold froid (m) FRW(ah) froide (f) FRW(ah)D

comb le peigne L(uh) P(ĕ)-NY(uh)

come (to) venir V(uh)-N(EE)R

company (business) la compagnie L(ah) K(O)ñ-P(ah)-NY(EE)

computer l'ordinateur L(O)R-D(EE)-N(ah)-T(ou)R

concert le concert L(uh) K(O)ñ-S(ĕ)R

condom le préservatif L(uh) PR(A)-Z(ĕ)R-V(ah)-T(EE)F

conference la conférence L(ah) K(O)ñ-F(A)-R(ah)ñS

conference room d'une salle de conférences D(ew)N S(ah)L D(uh) K(O)ñ-F(A)-R(ah)ñS

congratulations félicitations F(A)-L(EE)-S(EE)-T(ah)-S(EE)-(O)ñ

copy machine le copieur L(uh) K(O)-P(EE)-(ou)R

corn le maïs L(uh) M(ah)-(EE)S

cough syrup le sirop contre la toux
L(uh) S(ee)-R(o) K(o)ñ-TR(uh) L(ah) T(oo)

cover charge le couvert L(uh) K(oo)-V(ĕ)R

crab le crabe L(uh) KR(ah)B

cream la crème L(ah) KR(ĕ)M

credit card la carte de crédit
L(ah) K(ah)RT D(uh) KR(A)-D(ee)

cup la tasse L(ah) T(ah)S

customs la douane L(ah) DW(ah)N

D

dance (to) danser D(ah)ñ-S(A)

dangerous dangereux (m) D(ah)ñ-ZH(uh)-R(ou)
dangereuse (f) D(ah)ñ-ZH(uh)-R(ou)S

date (calendar) la date L(ah) D(ah)T

day le jour L(uh) ZH(oo)R

December décembre D(A)-S(ah)ñ-BR(uh)

delicious délicieux (m) D(A)-L(ee)-S(ee)-(ou)
délicieuse (f) D(A)-L(ee)-S(ee)-(ou)S

delighted enchanté (ah)ñ-SH(ah)ñ-T(A)

dentist le dentiste L(uh) D(ah)ñ-T(ee)ST

deodorant le déodorant L(uh) D(A)-(O)-D(O)-R(ah)ñ

department store le grand magasin
L(uh) GR(ah)ñ M(ah)-G(ah)-Z(ă)ñ

departure le départ L(uh) D(A)-P(ah)R

dessert le dessert L(uh) D(A)-S(ĕ)R

detour le détour L(uh) D(A)-T(oo)R

diabetic diabétique D(EE)-(ah)-B(A)-T(EE)K

diarrhea la diarrhée L(ah) D(EE)-(ah)-R(A)

dictionary le dictionnaire L(uh) D(EE)K-S(EE)-(O)-N(ĕ)R

dinner le dîner L(uh) D(EE)-N(A)

dining room la salle à manger
L(ah) S(ah)L (ah) M(ah)ñ-ZH(A)

direction la direction L(ah) D(EE)-R(ĕ)K-S(EE)-(O)ñ

dirty sale S(ah)L

disabled handicapé H(ah)ñ-D(EE)-K(ah)-P(A)

discount la remise L(ah) R(uh)-M(EE)Z

distance la distance L(ah) D(EE)S-T(ah)ñS

doctor le docteur L(uh) D(ah)K-T(ou)R

documents les documents (m)
L(A) D(O)-K(ew)-M(ah)ñ

dollar le dollar L(uh) D(O)-L(ah)R

down descendre D(ĕ)-S(ah)ñ-DR(uh)

downtown en ville (ah)ñ V(EE)L

dress la robe L(ah) R(O)B

drink (to) boire BW(ah)R

drive (to) conduire K(O)ñ-DW(EE)R

drugstore la pharmacie L(ah) F(ah)R-M(ah)-S(EE)

dry cleaner la teinturerie L(ah) T(ă)ñ-T(ew)-(ĕ)-R(EE)

duck le canard L(uh) K(ah)-N(ah)R

E

ear l'oreille L(O)-R(A)-Y(ou)

ear drops les gouttes pour les oreilles (f)
L(A) G(oo)T P(oo)R L(A) Z̲(O)-R(A)-Y(ou)

early tôt T(O)

east l'est (m) L(ĕ)ST

easy facile F(ah)-S(EE)L

eat (to) manger M(ah)ñ-ZH(A)

eggs l'oeuf L(ou)F

eggs (fried) les oeufs sur le plat (m/pl)
L(A) Z̲(ou)F S(ew)R L(uh) PL(ah)

eggs (scrambled) les oeufs brouillés (m/pl)
L(A) Z̲(ou)F BR(EE)-Y(A)

electricity l'électricité (f) LⒶ-LⓔK-TRⓔⓔ-Sⓔⓔ-TⒶ

elevator l'ascenseur (m) Lⓐⓗ-Sⓐⓗñ-SⓞⓤR

embassy l'ambassade (f) Lⓐⓗñ-Bⓐⓗ-SⓐⓗD

emergency l'urgence (f) LⓞⓤR-ZHⓐⓗñS

England l'Angleterre LⓐⓗNG-Lⓤⓗ-TⓔR

English anglais (m) ⓐⓗñ-GLⒶ

anglaise (f) ⓐⓗñ-GLⓔZ

enough C'est assez! SⒶ T̲ⓐⓗ-SⒶ

entrance l'entrée (f) Lⓐⓗñ-TR̰Ⓐ

envelope l'enveloppe (f) Lⓐⓗñ-Vⓤⓗ-LⓄP

evening la soirée Lⓐⓗ SWⓐⓗ-RⒶ

everything tout Tⓞⓞ

excellent excéllent (m) ⓔK-SⒶ-Lⓐⓗñ

excéllente (f) ⓔK-SⒶ-LⓐⓗñT

excuse me pardon PⓐⓗR-DⓄñ

exit la sortie Lⓐⓗ SⓄR-Tⓔⓔ

expensive cher SHⓔR

eyes les yeux (m) LⒶ Z̲ⓔⓔ-Yⓞⓤ

eyedrops les gouttes pour les yeux

LⒶ GⓞⓞT PⓞⓞR LⒶ Z̲ⓔⓔ-Yⓞⓤ

F

face le visage L(uh) V(EE)-S(ah)ZH

far loin LW(ă)ñ

fare (cost) le tarif L(uh) T(ah)-R(EE)F

fast rapide R(ah)-P(EE)D

fax le fax L(uh) F(ah)KS

fax machine d'un télécopieur
D(uh)ñ T(A)-L(A)-K(O)-P(EE)-(ou)R

February février F(A)-VR(EE)-(A)

few peu de P(ou) D(uh)

film (camera) la pellicule L(ah) P(ĕ)-L(EE)-K(ew)L

film (movie) le cinéma L(uh) S(EE)-N(A)-M(ah)

fine / very well très bien TR(A) B(EE)-(ă)ñ

finger le doigt L(uh) DW(ah)

fire! le feu! L(uh) F(ou)

fire extinguisher l'extincteur (m) L(ĕ)K-ST(ă)ñK-T(ou)R

first premier (m) PR(ĕ)M-Y(A)
premìère (f) PR(ĕ)M-Y(ĕ)R

fish le poisson L(uh) PW(ah)-S(O)ñ

flight le vol L(uh) V(O)L

florist shop le fleuriste L(uh) FL(ou)-R(EE)ST

flowers les fleurs L(A) FL(ou)R

food la nourriture L(ah) N(oo)-R(EE)-T(ew)R

foot le pied L(uh) PY(A)

fork la fourchette L(ah) F(oo)R-SH(ĕ)T

France la France L(ah) FR(ah)ñS

french fries les frites L(A) FR(EE)T

fresh frais FR(A)

Friday vendredi V(ah)ñ-DR(uh)-D(EE)

fried frit (m) FR(EE) frite (f) FR(EE)T

friend l'ami (m) L(ah)-M(EE) l'amie (f) L(ah)-M(EE)

fruit le fruit L(uh) FRW(EE)

funny drôle DR(O)L

G

gas station la station de service
L(ah) ST(ah)-S(EE)-(O)ñ D(uh) S(ĕ)R-V(EE)S

gasoline l'essence (f) L(ĕ)-S(ah)ñS

gate la barrière L(ah) B(ah)R-(EE)-(ĕ)R

gentleman monsieur M(uh)-SY(ou)

gift le cadeau L(uh) K(ah)-D(O)

girl la fille L(ah) F(EE)

glass (drinking) le verre L(uh) V(ĕ)R

glasses (eye) les lunettes LⒶ L(ew)-N(ĕ)T

gloves les gants LⒶ G(ah)ñ

gold l'or LⓄR

golf le golf L(uh) GⓄLF

golf course le terrain de golf
L(uh) T(ĕ)-R(ă)ñ D(ĕ) GⓄLF

good bon (m) BⓄñ bonne (f) B(uh)N

good-bye au revoir Ⓞ-R(uh)-VW(ah)R

grapes les raisins LⒶ RⒶ-Z(ă)ñ

grateful reconnaissant R(uh)-KⓄ-N(ĕ)-S(ah)ñ

gray gris (m) GR(ee) grise (f) GR(ee)S

green vert (m) V(ĕ)R verte (f) V(ĕ)RT

grocery store l'épicerie (f) LⒶ-P(ee)-S(ĕ)-R(ee)

group le groupe L(uh) GR(oo)P

guide le guide L(uh) G(ee)D

H

hair les cheveux (m/pl) LⒶ SH(uh)-V(ou)

hairbrush la brosse à cheveux
L(uh) BRⓄS (ah) SH(uh)-V(ou)

haircut la coupe de cheveux
L(ah) K(oo)P D(uh) SH(uh)-V(ou)

ham le jambon L(uh) ZH(ah)ñ-B(O)ñ

hamburger le hamburger L(uh) (ah)M-B(ĕ)R-G(ĕ)R

hand la main L(ah) M(ă)ñ

happy heureux (m) (ou)-R(ou)

heureuse (f) (ou)-R(ou)S

have (I) J'ai ZH(A)

he il (EE)L

head la tête L(ah) T(ĕ)T

headache mal à la tête M(ah) L̲(ah) L(ah) T(ĕ)T

health club le centre sportif

L(uh) S(ah)ñ-TR(uh) SP(O)R-T(EE)F

heart le coeur L(uh) K(ou)R

heart condition mal au coeur M(ah) L̲(O)-K(ou)R

heat la chaleur L(ah) SH(ah)-L(ou)R

hello bonjour B(O)ñ-ZH(oo)R

help au secours (O) S(uh)-K(oo)R

here ici (EE)-S(EE)

holiday la fête L(ah) F(ĕ)T

hospital l'hôpital (m) L(O)-P(EE)-T(ah)L

hot dog le hot dog L(uh) H(ah)T D(O)G

hotel l'hôtel (m) L(O)-T(ĕ)L

hour l'heure L(ou)R

how comment K(O)-M(O)ñ

hurry! dépêchez-vous! D(A)-P(ĕ)-SH(A) V(oo)

husband le marie (m) L(uh) M(ah)-R(EE)

I

I Je ZH(uh)

ice la glace L(ah) GL(ah)S

ice cream la glace L(ah) GL(ah)S

ice cubes le glaçons (f) L(A) GL(ah)-S(O)ñ

ill malade M(ah)-L(ah)D

important important (m) (ă)ñ-P(O)R-T(ah)ñ

importante (f) (ă)ñ-P(O)R-T(ah)ñT

indigestion la dyspepsie L(ah) D(EE)S-P(ĕ)P-S(EE)

information les renseignements (m)

L(A) R(ah)ñ-S(ĕ)N-Y(uh)-M(ah)ñ

inn l'auberge (f) L(O)-B(ĕ)RZH

interpreter l'interprète (m) L(ă)ñ-T(ĕ)R-PR(ĕ)T

J

jacket le veston L(uh) V(ĕ)S-T(O)ñ

jam la confiture L(ah) K(O)ñ-F(EE)-T(ew)R

January janvier ZH(ah)ñ-V(EE)-(A)

jewelry les bijoux (m) L(A) B(EE)-ZH(oo)

jewelry store la bijouterie L(ah) B(EE)-ZH(oo)-T(e)-R(EE)

job le travail L(uh) TR(ah)-V(ah)-Y(ou)

juice le jus L(uh) ZH(oo)

July juillet ZH(oo)-(EE)-(A)

June juin ZH(oo)-(ă)ñ

K

ketchup le ketchup L(uh) K(ĕ)-CH(uh)P

key la clé L(ah) KL(A)

kiss le baiser L(uh) B(A)-S(A)

knife le couteau L(uh) K(oo)-T(O)

know (I) Je sais ZH(uh) S(A)

L

ladies' restroom Dames D(ah)M

lady la dame L(ah) D(ah)M

lamb l'agneau L(ah)ñ-Y(O)

language la langue L(ah) L(ah)NG

large grand (m) GR(ah)ñ grande (f) GR(ah)ND

late tard T(ah)R

laundry la blanchisserie L(uh) BL(ah)ñ-SH(EE)-S(ĕ)-R(EE)

lawyer l'avocat (m) L(ah)-V(O)-K(ah)

left (direction) à gauche (f) (ah) G(O)SH

leg la jambe L(uh) ZH(ah)ñB

lemon le citron L(uh) S(EE)-TR(O)ñ

less moins MW(ă)ñ

letter la lettre L(ah) L(ĕ)-TR(uh)

lettuce la laitue L(ah) L(A)-T(ew)

light la lumière L(ah) L(ew)M-Y(ĕ)R

like comme K(O)M

like (I) Je veux ZH(uh) V(oo)

like (I would) Je voudrais ZH(uh) V(oo)-DR(A)

lip la lèvre L(ah) L(ĕ)-VR(uh)

lipstick le rouge L(uh) R(oo)ZH

little petit (m) P(uh)-T(EE) petite (f) P(uh)-T(EE)T

live (to) vivre V(EE)-VR(uh)

lobster le homard L(uh) (O)-M(ah)R

long long (m) L(O)ñ longue (f) L(O)NG

lost perdu P(ĕ)R-D(ew)

love l'amour L(ah)-M(oo)R

luck la chance L(ah) SH(ah)ñS

luggage les bagages (m) LⒶ Bⓐⓗ-Gⓐⓗ ZH

lunch le déjeuner Lⓤⓗ DⒶ-ZHⓞⓤ-NⒶ

M

maid la domestique Lⓐⓗ DⓄM-ⓔ̆S-TⒺⒺK

mail le courrier Lⓤⓗ Kⓞⓞ-RⒺⒺ-Ⓐ

makeup le maquillage Lⓤⓗ Mⓐⓗ-KⒺⒺ-Yⓐⓗ ZH

man l'homme (m) LⓄM

manager le gérant Lⓤⓗ ZHⒶ-Rⓐⓗñ

map le plan Lⓤⓗ PLⓐⓗñ

March mars Mⓐⓗ RS

market le marché Lⓤⓗ Mⓐⓗ R-SHⒶ

match (light) l'allumette (f) Lⓐⓗ-Lⓔⓦ-Mⓔ̆T

May mai MⒶ

mayonnaise la mayonnaise Lⓐⓗ Mⓐⓗ-YⓄ-Nⓔ̆Z

meal le repas Lⓤⓗ Rⓤⓗ-Pⓐⓗ

meat la viande Lⓐⓗ VⒺⒺ-ⓐⓗñD

mechanic le mécanicien Lⓤⓗ MⒶ-Kⓐⓗ-NⒺⒺ-SⒺⒺ-ⓐ̆ñ

medicine le médecine Lⓤⓗ MⒶ-Dⓤⓗ-SⒺⒺN

meeting le rendez-vous Lⓤⓗ Rⓐⓗñ-DⒶ-Vⓞⓞ

mens' restroom messieurs Mⓔ̆-SYⓞⓤ

menu la carte Lⓐⓗ Kⓐⓗ RT

message le message L(uh) M(ĕ)-S(ah)-ZH

milk le lait L(uh) L(A)

mineral water l'eau minérale (f) L(O) M(EE)-N(A)-R(ah)L

minute le minute L(uh) M(EE)-N(ew)T

Miss mademoiselle M(ah)D-MW(ah)-Z(ĕ)L

mistake la faute L(ah) F(O)T

misunderstanding le malentendu
L(uh) M(ah)L-(ah)ñ-T(ah)ñ-D(ew)

moment le moment L(uh) M(O)-M(ah)ñ

Monday lundi L(uh)ñ-D(EE)

money l'argent (m) L(ah)R-ZH(ah)ñ

month le mois L(uh) MW(ah)

monument le monument L(uh) M(O)-N(ew)-M(ah)ñ

more plus PL(ew)

morning le matin L(uh) M(ah)-T(ă)ñ

mosque la mosquée L(ah) M(O)S-K(A)

mother la mère L(ah) M(ĕ)R

mountain la montagne L(ah) M(O)ñ-T(ah)N-Y(uh)

movie le cinéma L(uh) S(EE)-N(A)-M(ah)

Mr. monsieur M(uh)-SY(ou)

Mrs. madame M(ah)-D(ah)M

much (too) trop TR(O)

museum le musée L(uh) M(ew)-Z(A)

mushroom le champignon L(uh) SH(ah)ñ-P(EE)N-Y(O)N

music la musique L(ah) M(ew)-Z(EE)K

mustard la moutarde L(ah) M(oo)-T(ah)RD

N

nail polish la vernis à ongles
L(ah) V(ĕ)R-N(EE) S̲(ah) (O)ñ-GL(uh)

name le nom L(uh) N(O)ñ

napkin la serviette L(ah) S(ĕ)R-V(EE)-(ĕ)T

near près de PR(A) D(uh)

neck le cou L(uh) K(oo)

need (I) J'ai besoin ZH(A) B(uh)-ZW(ă)ñ

never jamais ZH(ah)-M(A)

newspaper le journal L(uh) ZH(oo)R-N(ah)L

news stand le kiosque L(uh) K(EE)-(ah)SK

night la nuit L(ah) NW(EE)

nightclub la boite de nuit L(ah) BW(ah)T D(uh) NW(EE)

no non N(O)ñ

no smoking non fumeurs N(O)ñ F(ew)-M(ou)R

noon midi M(EE)-D(EE)

north le nord L(uh) NⓄR

notary le notaire L(uh) NⓄ-T(ĕ)R

November novembre NⓄ-V(ah)ñ-BR(uh)

now maintenant M(ă)ñ-T(uh)-N(ah)ñ

number le numéro L(uh) N(ew)-MⒶ-RⓄ

nurse l'infirmière (f) L(ă)ñ-F(EE)R-M(EE)-(ĕ)R

O

occupied occupé Ⓞ-K(ew)-PⒶ

ocean l'océan (m) LⓄ-SⒶ-(ah)ñ

October octobre ⓄK-TⓄ-BR(uh)

officer l'officier (m) LⓄ-F(EE)-S(EE)-Ⓐ

oil l'huile (f) L(ew)-(EE)L

omelet l'omelette (f) LⓄM-L(ĕ)T

one way (traffic) sens unique S(ah)ñS (ew)-N(EE)K

onions les oignons LⒶ Z̲Ⓞ-NYⓄñ

open (to) ouvrir (oo)-VR(EE)R

opera l'opéra (m) LⓄ-PⒶ-R(ah)

operator le standardiste L(uh) ST(ah)N-D(ah)R-D(EE)ST

optician l'opticien LⓄP-T(EE)-S(EE)-(ă)ñ

orange (color) orange Ⓞ-R(ah)ñ-ZH

orange (fruit) l'orange (f) LⓄ-R(ah)ñZH

order (to) commander KⓄ-M(ah)ñ-DⒶ

original original Ⓞ-R(EE)-ZH(EE)-N(ah)L

owner le propriétaire L(uh) PRⓄ-PR(EE)-Y(ĕ)-T(ĕ)R

oysters les huîtres (f/pl) LⒶ Z̲W(EE)-TR(uh)

P

package le paquet L(uh) P(ah)-K(ĕ)

paid payé PⒶ-YⒶ

pain la douleur L(ah) D(oo)-L(ou)R

painting la peinture L(ah) P(ă)ñ-T(ew)R

pantyhose le collant L(uh) KⓄ-L(ah)ñ

paper le papier L(uh) P(ah)-P(EE)-Ⓐ

park (to) stationner ST(ah)-S(EE)-Ⓞ-NⒶ

park le parc L(uh) P(ah)RK

partner (business) associé (ah)-SⓄ-S(EE)-Ⓐ

party la soirée L(ah) SW(ah)-RⒶ

passenger le passager L(uh) P(ah)-S(ah)-ZHⒶ

passport le passeport L(uh) P(ah)S-PⓄR

pasta les pâtes LⒶ P(ah)T

pastries les pâtisseries L(ah) P(ah)-T(EE)-S(ĕ)-R(EE)

pen le stylo L(uh) ST(EE)-L(O)

pencil le crayon L(uh) KR(A)-Y(O)ñ

pepper le poivre L(uh) PW(ah)-VR(uh)

perfume le parfum L(uh) P(ah)R-F(uh)ñ

person la personne L(ah) P(ĕ)R-S(O)N

person to person de communication avec préavis D(uh) K(O)-M(ew)-N(EE)-K(ah)-S(EE)-(O)ñ (ah)-V(ĕ)K PR(A)-(ah)-V(EE)

pharmacist le pharmacien L(uh) F(ah)R-M(ah)-S(EE)-(ă)ñ

pharmacy la pharmacie L(ah) F(ah)R-M(ah)-S(EE)

phone book l'annuaire L(ah)-N(ew)-(ĕ)R

photo la photo L(A) F(O)-T(O)

photographer le photographier L(uh) F(O)-T(O)-GR(ah)-F(EE)-(A)

pie la tarte L(ah) T(ah)RT

pillow l'oreiller (m) L(O)-R(A)-Y(A)

pink rose R(O)Z

pizza la pizza L(ah) P(EE)D-S(ah)

plastic le plastique L(uh) PL(ah)S-T(EE)K

plate l'assiette (f) L(ah)-S(EE)-(ĕ)T

please s'il vous plaît S(EE)L V(oo) PL(ĕ)

pleasure le plaisir L(uh) PL(ĕ)-Z(EE)R

police la police L(ah) P(O)-L(EE)S

police station la poste de police
L(ah) P(O)ST D(uh) P(uh)-L(EE)S

pork le porc L(uh) P(O)R

porter le porteur L(uh) P(O)R-T(ou)R

post office la poste L(ah) P(O)ST

postcard la carte postale L(ah) K(ah)RT P(O)S-T(ah)L

potato la pomme de terre L(ah) P(uh)M D(uh) T(ĕ)R

pregnant enceinte (ah)ñ-S(ă)ñT

prescription la prescription L(ah) PR(ĕ)-SKR(EE)P-S(EE)-(O)ñ

price le prix L(uh) PR(EE)

problem le problème L(uh) PR(O)-BL(ĕ)M

profession la profession L(ah) PR(O)-F(ĕ)-S(EE)-(O)N

public publique P(ew)B-L(EE)K

public telephone le téléphone publique
L(uh) T(A)-L(A)-F(O)N P(ew)B-L(EE)K

purified purifié P(ew)R-(EE)-F(EE)-(A)

purple violet (m) V(EE)-(O)-L(A)
violette (f) V(EE)-(O)-L(ĕ)T

purse le sac L(uh) S(ah)K

Q

quality la qualité L(ah) K(ah)-L(EE)-TⒶ

question la question L(ah) K(ĕ)S-T(EE)-Ⓞñ

quickly rapidement R(ah)-P(EE)D-M(ah)ñ

quiet (be) taisez-vous TⒶ-ZⒶ V(oo)

quiet tranquille TR(ah)ñ-K(EE)L

R

radio la radio L(ah) R(ah)D-YⓄ

railroad le chemin de fer L(uh) SH(uh)-M(ă)ñ D(uh) F(ĕ)R

rain la pluie L(ah) PL(ew)-(EE)

raincoat l'imperméable (m) L(ă)ñ-P(ĕ)R-MⒶ-(ah)B-L(uh)

ramp la rampe L(ah) R(ah)MP

rare (cooked) saignant SⒶ-NY(ah)ñ

razor blades les lames de rasoir
LⒶ L(ah)M D(uh) R(ah)-SW(ah)R

ready prêt PR(ĕ)

receipt le reçu L(uh) R(uh)-S(ew)

recommend (to) recommander R(uh)-KⓄ-M(ah)ñ-DⒶ

red rouge R(oo)ZH

repeat répéter RⒶ-PⒶ-TⒶ

reservation la réservation L(ah) R(A)-Z(ĕ)R-V(ah)-S(EE)-(O)ñ

restaurant le restaurant L(uh) R(ĕ)S-T(O)-R(ah)ñ

return revenir R(uh)-V(uh)-N(EE)R

return (to give back) revenir R(uh)-V(uh)-N(EE)R

rice le riz L(uh) R(EE)

rich riche R(EE)SH

right (correct) correct K(O)-R(ĕ)KT

right (direction) à droite (ah) DRW(ah)T

road le chemin L(uh) SH(uh)-M(ă)ñ

room la chambre L(ah) SH(ah)ñ-BR(uh)

round trip l'aller et retour L(ah)-L(A) (A) R(uh)-T(oo)R

S

safe (hotel) le coffre-fort L(uh) K(O)-FR(uh) F(O)R

salad la salade L(ah) S(ah)-L(ah)D

sale la vente L(ah) V(ah)ñT

salmon le saumon L(uh) S(O)-M(O)ñ

salt le sel L(uh) S(ĕ)L

sandwich le sandwich L(uh) S(ah)ñ-W(EE)CH

Saturday samedi S(ah)-M(uh)-D(EE)

scissors les ciseaux (m) L(A) S(EE)-Z(O)

sculpture la sculpture L(ah) SK(ew)LP-T(ew)R

seafood les fruits de mer (m) L(A) FRW(EE) D(uh) M(ĕ)R

season la saison L(ah) S(ĕ)-Z(O)ñ

seat la place L(ah) PL(ah)S

secretary la secrétaire L(ah) S(ĕ)-KR(A)-T(ĕ)R

section la section L(ah) S(ĕ)K-S(EE)-(oo)ñ

September septembre S(ĕ)P-T(ah)ñ-BR(uh)

service le service L(uh) S(ĕ)R-V(EE)S

several plusieurs PL(ew)-ZY(ou)R

shampoo le shampooing L(uh) SH(ah)ñ-P(oo)-(ă)N

sheets (bed) les draps L(A) DR(ah)

shirt la chemise L(ah) SH(uh)-M(EE)S

shoe la chaussure L(ah) SH(O)-S(ew)R

shoe store la boutique de chaussures
L(ah) B(oo)-T(EE)K D(uh) SH(O)-S(ew)R

shop la boutique L(ah) B(oo)-T(EE)K

shopping center le centre commercial
L(uh) S(ah)ñ-TR(uh) K(O)-M(ĕ)R-S(EE)-(ah)L

shower la douche L(ah) D(oo)SH

shrimp les crevettes L(A) KR(uh)-V(ĕ)T

sick malade M(ah)-L(ah)D

sign (display) le signe L(uh) S(EE)N-Y(uh)

signature la signature L(ah) S(EE)N-Y(ah)-T(ew)R

single seul S(ou)L

sir monsieur M(uh)-SY(ou)

sister la soeur L(ah) S(ou)R

size la taille L(ah) TⒶ-Y(ou)

skin la peau LⒶ PⓄ

skirt la jupe L(ah) ZH(oo)P

sleeve la manche L(ah) M(ah)ñSH

slowly lentement L(ah)ñ-T(uh)-M(ah)ñ

small petit (m) P(uh)-T(EE)

petite (f) P(uh)-T(EE)T

smile (to) sourire S(oo)-R(EE)R

smoke (to) fumer F(ew)-MⒶ

soap le savon L(uh) S(ah)-VⓄñ

sock les chaussettes LⒶ SHⓄ-S(ĕ)T

some quelque K(ĕ)L-K(uh)

something quelque chose K(ĕ)L-K(uh) SHⓄZ

sometimes quelquefois K(ĕ)L-K(uh)-FW(ah)

soon bientôt B(EE)-(ă)ñ-TⓄ

sorry (I am) Je suis désolé ZH(uh) SW(EE) DⒶ-SⓄ-LⒶ

soup la soupe L(ah) S(oo)P

south le sud L(uh) S(ew)D

souvenir le souvenir L(uh) S(oo)-V(uh)-N(EE)R

speciality la spécialité L(ah) SPⒶ-S(EE)-(ah)-L(EE)-TⒶ

spoon la cuillère L(ah) KW(EE)-(ĕ)R

spring (season) le printemps L(uh) PR(ă)ñ-T(ah)ñ

stairs les escaliers LⒶ Z̲(ĕ)-SK(ah)L-YⒶ

stamp le timbre L(uh) T(ă)ñ-BR(uh)

station la gare L(ah) G(ah)R

steak le bifteck L(uh) B(EE)F-T(ĕ)K

steamed à l'etuvée (ah) LⒶ-T(ew)-VⒶ

stop arrêtez (ah)-R(ĕ)-TⒶ

store le magasin L(uh) M(ah)-G(ah)-Z(ă)ñ

straight ahead tout droit T(oo) DRW(ah)

strawberry la fraise L(ah) FR(ĕ)Z

street la rue L(ah) R(ew)

string la ficelle L(ah) F(EE)-S(ĕ)L

subway le métro L(uh) MⒶ-TRⓄ

sugar le sucre L(uh) S(ew)-KR(uh)

suit (clothes) le complet L(uh) KⓄñ-PL(ĕ)

suitcase la valise L(ah) V(ah)-L(EE)S

summer l'été LⒶ-TⒶ

sun le soleil L(uh) S(O)-L(A)

Sunday dimanche D(EE)-M(ah)ñSH

sunglasses les lunettes de soleil (f)
L(A) L(ew)-N(ĕ)T D(uh) S(O)-L(A)

suntan lotion la lotion à bronzer
L(ah) L(O)-S(EE)-(O)ñ (ah) BR(O)ñ-Z(A)

supermarket le supermarché
L(uh) S(ew)-P(ĕ)R-M(ah)R-SH(A)

surprise la surprise L(ah) S(ew)R-PR(EE)Z

sweet doux D(oo)

swim (to) nager N(ah)-ZH(A)

swimming pool la piscine L(ah) P(EE)-S(EE)N

synagogue la synagogue L(ah) S(EE)-N(ah)-G(O)G

T

table la table L(ah) T(ah)-BL(uh)

tampons les tampons L(A) T(ah)ñ-P(O)ñ

tape (sticky) le ruban L(uh) R(ew)-B(ah)ñ

tape recorder le magnétophone
L(uh) M(ah)-N(A)-T(O)-F(O)N

tax la taxe L(ah) T(ah)KS

taxi le taxi L⓾ T㊊K-S㊍

tea le thé L⓾ TⒶ

telegram le télégramme L⓾ TⒶ-LⒶ-GR㊊M

telephone le téléphone L⓾ TⒶ-LⒶ-FⓄN

television la télévision L㊊ TⒶ-LⒶ-V㊍-S㊍-Ⓞñ

temperature la température L㊊ T㊊ñ-PⒺ-R㊊-T㊎R

temple le temple L⓾ T㊊ñ-PL⓾

tennis la tennis L㊊ TⒺ-N㊍S

tennis court le terrain de tennis

L⓾ TⒺ-RⒶñ D⓾ TⒺ-N㊍S

thank you merci MⒺR-S㊍

that cela S⓾-L㊊

the le (m) L⓾

la (f) L㊊

theater le théâtre L⓾ TⒶ-㊊-TR⓾

there là L㊊

they ils ㊍L

this ce / cet / cette S⓾ / SⒺT / SⒺT

thread le fil L⓾ F㊍L

throat la gorge L㊊ GⓄRZH

Thursday jeudi ZH㊐-D㊍

ticket le billet L(uh) B(EE)-YⒶ

tie la cravate L(ah) KR(ah)-V(ah)T

time l'heure L(ou)R

tip (gratuity) le pourboire L(uh) P(oo)R-BW(ah)R

tire (car) le pneu L(uh) P(uh)-N(ou)

tired fatigué F(ah)-T(EE)-GⒶ

toast pain grillé P(ah)ñ GR(EE)-YⒶ

tobacco le tabac L(uh) T(ah)-B(ah)

today aujourd'hui ⓄH-ZH(oo)R-DW(EE)

toe l'orteil LⓄR-TⒶ

together ensemble (ah)ñ-S(ah)ñ-BL(uh)

toilet la toilette L(ah) TW(ah)-L(ĕ)T

toilet paper le papier hygiénique

L(uh) P(ah)-P(EE)-Ⓐ (EE)-ZH(EE)-Ⓐ-N(EE)K

tomato la tomate L(ah) TⓄ-M(ah)T

tomorrow demain D(uh)-M(ă)ñ

toothache le mal aux dents L(uh) M(ah)L Ⓞ D(ah)ñ

toothbrush la brosse à dents L(ah) BRⓄS (ah) D(ah)ñ

toothpaste le dentifrice L(uh) D(ah)ñ-T(EE)-FR(EE)S

toothpick le cure-dents L(uh) K(ew)R D(ah)ñ

tour la visite L(ah) V(EE)-Z(EE)T

tourist le touriste L(uh) T(oo)-R(EE)ST

tourist office le bureau de tourisme L(uh) B(ew)-R(O) D(uh) T(oo)-R(EE)S-M(uh)

towel la serviette L(ah) S(ĕ)R-V(EE)-(ĕ)T

train le train L(uh) TR(ă)ñ

travel agency l'agence de voyage L(ah)-ZH(ah)ñS D(uh) VW(ah)-Y(ah)ZH

traveler's check le chèque de voyage L(uh) SH(ĕ)K D(uh) VW(ah)-Y(ah)ZH

trip le voyage L(uh) VW(ah)-Y(ah)ZH

trousers le pantalon L(uh) P(ah)ñ-T(ah)-L(O)ñ

trout la truite L(ah) TRW(ew)-(EE)T

truth la vérité L(ah) V(A)-R(EE)-T(A)

Tuesday mardi M(ah)R-D(EE)

turkey la dinde L(ah) D(ă)ñND

U

umbrella la parapluie L(ah) P(ah)-R(ah)-PL(ew)-(EE)

understand (to) comprendre K(O)N-PR(ah)ñ-DR(uh)

undestand les sous-vêtements L(A) S(oo) V(ĕ)T-M(ah)ñ

United Kingdom Royaume-Uni R(oy)-(oo)M (oo)-N(EE)

United States les Etats-Unis LⒶ Z̲Ⓐ-Tⓐⓗ-Z̲ⓔⓦ-NⒺⒺ

university l'université (f) Lⓔⓦ-NⒺⒺ-Vⓔ̆R-SⒺⒺ-TⒶ

up haut Ⓞ

urgent urgent ⓔⓦR-ZHⓐⓗñ

V

vacancies (accommodation) chambres libres (f)
SHⓐⓗñ-BRⓤⓗ LⒺⒺ-BRⓤⓗ

vacation les vacances LⒶ Vⓐⓗ-KⓐⓗñS

valuable précieux (m) PRⒶ-SYⓞⓤ
précieuse (f) PRⒶ-SYⓞⓤS

value le valeur Lⓤⓗ Vⓐⓗ-LⓞⓤR

vanilla la vanille Lⓐⓗ Vⓐⓗ-NⒺⒺ

veal le veau Lⓤⓗ VⓄ

vegetables les légumes (m) LⒶ LⒶ-GⓔⓦM

view la vue Lⓐⓗ Vⓔⓦ

vinegar le vinaigre Lⓤⓗ VⒺⒺ-NⒶ-GRⓤⓗ

voyage le voyage Lⓤⓗ VWⓐⓗ-YⓐⓗZH

W

wait attendez ⓐⓗ-Tⓐⓗñ-DⒶ

waiter le garçon Lⓤⓗ GⓐⓗR-SⓄñ

waitress la serveuse Lⓐⓗ Sⓔ̆R-VⓞⓤS

want (I) Je voudrais ZH(uh) V(oo)-DR(A)

wash (to) laver L(ah)-V(A)

watch (time piece) la montre L(ah) M(O)ñ-TR(uh)

watch out! attention (ah)-T(ah)ñ-S(EE)-(O)ñ

water l'eau L(O)

we nous N(oo)

weather le temps L(uh) T(ah)ñ

Wednesday mercredi M(ĕ)R-KR(uh)-D(EE)

week la semaine L(ah) S(uh)-M(ĕ)N

weekend le week-end L(uh) W(EE)K-(ĕ)ND

welcome bienvenu B(EE)-(ă)ñ-V(ĕ)-N(ew)

well done (cooked) bien cuit B(EE)-(ă)ñ KW(EE)

west l'ouest L(oo)-(ĕ)ST

what? que? / quoi? K(uh) / KW(ah)

wheelchair le fauteuil roulant

L(uh) F(O)-T(ou)-Y(ou) R(oo)-L(ah)ñ

when? quand? K(ah)ñ

where? où? (oo)

which? quel? / quelle K(ĕ)L

white blanc (m) BL(ah)ñ blanche (f) BL(ah)ñSH

who? qui? K(EE)

why? pourquoi? P(oo)R-KW(ah)

wife la femme L(ah) F(ah)M

wind le vent L(uh) V(ah)ñ

window la fenêtre L(ah) F(uh)-N(ĕ)-TR(uh)

wine le vin L(uh) V(ă)ñ

wine list la carte de vins L(ah) K(ah)RT D(uh) V(ă)ñ

winter l'hiver L(EE)-V(ĕ)R

with avec (ah)-V(ĕ)K

woman la femme L(ah) F(ah)M

wonderful merveilleux M(ĕ)R-V(A)-Y(ou)

world le monde L(uh) M(O)ñD

wrong avoir tort (uh)-VW(ah)R T(O)R

XYZ

year l'année L(ah)-N(A)

yellow jaune ZH(O)N

yes oui W(EE)

yesterday hier Y(ĕ)R

you tu / vous T(ew) / V(oo)

zipper la fermeture L(ah) F(ĕ)R-M(uh)-T(ew)R

zoo le zoo L(uh) Z(O)

THANKS!

The nicest thing you can say to anyone in any language is "Thank you." Try some of these languages using the incredible EPLS Vowel Symbol System.

Spanish	**French**
GR(ah)´-S(EE)-(ah)S	M(ĕ)R-S(EE)
German	**Italian**
D(ah)´N-K(uh)	GR(ah)´T-S(EE)-(ĕ)
Japanese	**Chinese**
D(O)-M(O)	SH(EE)(ĕ) SH(EE)(ĕ)

Swedish T(ah)K	**Portuguese** (O)-BR(EE)-G(ah)-D(O)
Arabic SH(oo)-KR(ah)N	**Greek** (ĕ)F-H(ah)-R(EE)-ST(O)
Hebrew T(O)-D(ah)	**Russian** SP(ah)-S(EE)-B(ah)
Swahili (ah)-S(ah)N-T(A)	**Dutch** D(ah)NK (oo)
Tagalog S(ah)-L(ah)-M(ah)T	**Hawaiian** M(ah)-H(ah)-L(O)

INDEX

NOTES

QUICK REFERENCE PAGE

Hello
Bonjour
B(O)ñ ZH(oo)R

Good-bye
Au revoir
(O) R(uh)-VW(ah)R

How are you?
Comment allez-vous?
K(O)-M(O)ñ T(ah)-L(A)-V(oo)

Fine / Very well
Très bien
TR(A) B(EE)-(ă)ñ

Yes
Oui
W(EE)

No
Non
N(O)ñ

Please
S'il vous plaît
S(EE)L V(oo) PL(ĕ)

Thank you
Merci
M(ĕ)R-S(EE)

I would like...
Je voudrais...
ZH(uh) V(oo)-DR(A)...

Where is...
Où est...
(oo) (A)...

I don't understand!
Je ne comprends pas!
ZH(uh)N-(uh) K(O)ñ-PR(ah)ñ P(ah)

Help!
Au secours!
(O) S(uh)-K(oo)R